USE PROTECTION

An Employee's Guide to
Advancement in the Workplace

Johanna Harris

Printed by CreateSpace
Available from Amazon.com, CreateSpace.com,
and other retail outlets
Available on Kindle and other devices
Cover design by Luke Harris
ISBN-13: 978-1492961840
ISBN-10: 1492961841

To Jeff, Zoe and Luke

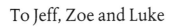

DISCLAIMERS

This book contains numerous brief vignettes that are intended to illustrate many of the key points of the text. The circumstances described in these vignettes, including the names of characters and business firms, are fictitious. Any resemblance to real persons, living or dead, or to real business entities, past or present, is purely coincidental.

USE PROTECTION is addressed to employees in a non-union workplace. If you work in a unionized company, there will be separate sets of rules, procedures and laws that will apply to you.

CONTENTS

INTRODUCTION

Whether you're just starting your career or are somewhere beyond that, your most important goals are to find what you're good at, determine what kind of work you want to do and invest in yourself. The purpose of *USE PROTECTION* is to make sure you understand enough about workplace practices and employment law so that you don't get derailed from the track you should be on.

Many of the rules that govern work in any organization, whether it's a large corporation or a two-man office, are not obvious. Some may be counterintuitive. If you don't know what the rules are, they can tangle you in a knot. At the very least, you'll waste valuable time and energy getting yourself untangled. That's time and energy better spent on your career.

You may be thinking that your company has a human resources person who will keep you out of trouble. This is a dangerous misconception. Whether your company has a massive Human Resources Department with hundreds of representatives or a small office with just a single representative, these HR reps are not your advocates. They work for the company, not for you. The company evaluates and pays them for pursuing management's interest. Some human resources representatives are skilled at ensuring that managers obey personnel laws and adhere to company policies. They appear to be acting in your interest. But they are not your advocates. You must be your own advocate. You must protect yourself.

USE PROTECTION covers fifteen key topics that you need to pay attention to. You need to know enough about these topics to protect yourself.

1. JOB INTERVIEWS: As a job applicant, you might be asked questions that are improper or illegal. You need to figure out in advance how to respond to these questions. Don't assume that you'll have some effective legal recourse if it turns out that you weren't hired because of your answer to an improper question.

2. OFFER LETTERS: Your offer letter contains provisions that will have a big impact on the quality of your life while you're on the job and even after you've left the job. You need to know what these provisions mean and whether in some cases you can negotiate a better deal for yourself.

3. BACKGROUND INVESTIGATIONS: Your employer has enormous leeway in what it can find out about you. If there are problems in your background, they are likely to be discovered during the application process. Before you apply for a job, you need to fix whatever problems you can.

4. MENTORING: Quite often the most important things that will allow you to advance in your career are not written down. A mentor can serve as a valuable source of this unwritten code. Don't expect your manager to clue you in.

5. PERFORMANCE EVALUATIONS: A performance evaluation can be a valuable tool that allows you to showcase your accomplishments and receive useful feedback. But it can also highlight an unfair assessment on you manager's part. You need to understand how an evaluation can be unfair and what to do about it.

6. OVERTIME PAY: You may be entitled to overtime pay. Unfortunately, in these tight economic times, your

employer may be reluctant to pay you overtime. It may even ask you to forgo overtime if you want to keep your job. When it comes to overtime pay, you need to know your rights.

7. FAMILY MEDICAL LEAVE ACT: During the course of your employment, you or a family member may become pregnant, ill or injured. You don't want to lose your job because you had to leave work to care for yourself or someone else. Knowing your legal rights to be absent from work can save your job.

8. DISABILITIES: If you need help in performing your job because of a disability, you should ask for help. Your employer is legally obligated to make a reasonable effort to ensure you have what you need to do your work.

9. INVESTIGATIONS: Your company has enormous scope in investigating potential wrongdoing by its employees. Don't be blindsided when your company uncovers something that you thought was hidden or inaccessible.

10. SEXUAL HARASSMENT: You need to understand exactly what constitutes sexual harassment. The last thing you need is to be caught up in an investigation of something you did or said. Once you understand what is sexual harassment, don't do it.

11. WORKPLACE VIOLENCE: Likewise, you need to understand exactly what constitutes workplace violence. You don't want to do anything that could trigger an investigation of your conduct. So again, once you understand what is considered workplace violence, don't engage in it.

12. TERMINATION FOR POOR JOB PERFORMANCE: If you're having problems doing your job, there are important steps that you can take before you get fired.

13. TERMINATION FOR VIOLATION OF COMPANY POLICIES: You need to know the rules of your company and follow them no matter how absurd they appear. Your company has the right to fire you for a wide range of actions that it believes to be contrary to its interests. The fact that you broke a silly rule may turn out to be irrelevant.

14. REDUCTIONS IN FORCE: If your employer engages in a reduction in force (or RIF), you may be terminated through no fault of your own. If there is a RIF in your company, you need to know how management determines who stays and who goes. It may save you your job.

15. NON-COMPETE AND NON-SOLICITATION AGREEMENTS: These agreements can affect your ability to get a new job after you leave your current job. You need to understand the pitfalls and stumbling blocks in

these agreements so that you can full advantage of your next job offer.

A note on pronouns

Throughout USE PROTECTION, the reader is addressed as "you." This doesn't necessarily imply that the facts describe your situation. For ease of exposition, the male pronoun "he" is used to avoid repeatedly referring to "he or she."

1. JOB INTERVIEWS

This chapter will not advise you to arrive on time at your job interview, to wear clean clothes or to make eye contact with your interviewer when you shake his hand. You know all that already.

Instead, this chapter prepares you for the questions you may be asked during the interview, because the answers can win or lose a job for you. Before you walk through the door and shake the interviewer's hand, you need to anticipate what questions will be asked and have a strategy already prepared for your appropriate and compelling answers.

Keep in mind the interviewer's principal goals. He will obviously want to ask in-depth questions about your skills and experience. But even more important, the interview is an opportunity to assess whether you are a team player, can take direction, can control your emotions, can solve problems and be loyal to your employer.

Inappropriate or illegal interview questions

Unfortunately, employers will sometimes ask you certain questions that they should not ask. These questions could elicit information, such as your nationality or race, that an employer is not legally entitled to use in deciding whether to hire you. When you're asked such a question, you are caught between a rock and a hard place. A claim you did not get a job because of an illegal question is almost impossible to prove. Pointing out to the interviewer that the question is improper will guarantee you will never hear from him again.

The best advice is to figure out what the interviewer is really interested in and attempt to address his concern in an appropriate, convincing manner. If that's not possible, then you can respond to a specific question with general, impersonal information. More on that shortly.

It is important to be truthful in providing information on your skills, education and job history. But it is not necessary for you to provide truthful information about matters that are neither job related nor legally permissible.

However, if you think an improper question reveals something deeply troubling about the culture of the organization, make a graceful exit and cross the company off your list of potential employers.

Some questions that an interviewer cannot legally ask you

• How old are you? When do you plan to retire? What year did you graduate from high school?

58-year-old Wilma is applying for a position in the healthcare field that will require extensive on-the-job training. The interviewer asks, "When did you graduate from high school?" Wilma could respond, "My last two positions required extensive training in electronic medical records and billing. I successfully completed both training programs, and I look forward to completing the required training modules for this job." This answer refocuses the interview from the inappropriate issue of Wilma's age to the more relevant question about her ability to learn new skills.

• What is your race? What is your religion? Where are you from? What is your national origin? What religious holidays do you observe?

Julia's father is Thai and her mother is Brazilian. The interviewer comments on Julia's "exotic looks," and asks her "Where are you from?" Julia could respond, "Thank you. For as long as I can remember, people have been telling me that I look just like my mother, who in turn looks like her mother." The idea behind Julia's answer is not to permit the interviewer to resort to ill-conceived stereotypes about Asians or Latin Americans.

- Is English your first language?

Jeffrey grew up in a Spanish-speaking household and learned English in primary school. The interviewer asks, "What is your native tongue?" Jeffrey could respond, "I am bilingual. I have taken all required college entrance exams – including reading and writing – in both English and Spanish." This answer addresses the issue that the interviewer should have focused on, namely, Jeffrey's ability to write work-related memos in competent English.

- Are you married? Do you have reliable child care? Are you responsible for any sick or elderly relatives?

Rhea, a 28-year-old woman, is applying for a managerial position that entails daily deadlines. The interviewer asks, "What personal and family obligations do you have?" Rhea could reply, "There's nothing in my life that would prevent me from showing up for work every single day. In fact, every job I've had thus far has involved remaining at work after 5 p.m. to meet tight deadlines." An employer has a legitimate interest in determining whether you are able to show up and stay until the work is done. But it is your right to determine how you conduct your life in order to fulfill these obligations. It is not your employer's business what relationships or obligations you have.

• Do you drink? Have you ever had a problem with alcohol or drugs? Do you have any chronic conditions, such as asthma or migraines? Have you ever had cancer? Have you ever filed for workers compensation or disability pay as a result of an injury?

> *Barry's resume shows a two-year gap between jobs. In fact, Barry had a back injury, became dependent on painkillers and subsequently underwent rehabilitation. The interviewer asks him, "Was the two-year lapse between jobs a result of a medical problem?" Barry could respond, "Over the last few years, I've tried work in several different areas, but more recently, I've settled into this particular field. I am fully capable of carrying out the responsibilities of this job without any complications of any kind." Employers are categorically forbidden to ask questions about an applicant's health. Any questions in this area should be directed to the particular duties required of the job. An employer could legally inquire, "This job entails transferring patients from one bed to another. Can you do that?" or "This job entails cross-country air travel to our field office. Can you do that?"*

• What is your sexual orientation? Are you gay? Are you lesbian? Do you have a same-sex partner?

Once gay marriage became legal in his state of residence, Xavier married his long-time partner Tyler. The interviewer asks Xavier, "Who do you live with?" Xavier could respond, "I was recently able to buy a beautiful colonial just to the west of the city. The schools are excellent and there's a huge back yard for my Irish terrier." The sexual orientation of an employee has no bearing on any job duties and should not be the topic of discussion.

- Have you been divorced? Do you pay alimony or child support?

Jordan is the divorced father of four children. He pays both alimony and child support. He has been remarried for five years and has two stepchildren. The interviewer asks Jordan, "Do you have any financial obligations outside your current family?" Jordan could respond, "My wife and I are able to provide comfortably for our family."

- Have you ever sued your employer?

Stephanie was the victim of race discrimination by her previous employer. She filed a discrimination complaint, which was written up in the local newspaper. Referring to the article, the interviewer asks Stephanie, "What happened?" Stephanie could respond, "It is true that my former manager and I had some disagreements, but fortunately these disagreements were resolved to everyone's satisfaction." Stephanie's new employer cannot refuse to hire her because she sued a former employer.

Her best course of action is to minimize the prior conflict, without offering any details.

● Have you or anyone in your family ever joined a labor union?

Carl's father was the president of local pipe fitter's union for many years. The interviewer asks Carl, "Are you from a union family?" Carl could respond, "I am very proud of the long tradition of hard-working men and women in my family. While my brothers, sisters and I were growing up, my father worked two jobs to save for college tuitions. My mother went back to work as a librarian after we finished high school."

Some legal interview questions that you need to anticipate

Many interview questions may appear personal, but they are nonetheless legal. The key is to have your answers formulated in advance, so that you're not composing them on the spot.

● Are you legally able to work in the United States?

● Can you travel if the job requires it?

Travel is stressful and requires your being away from your family. It's not for everyone. You had better decide in advance if you're willing to travel. If so, the correct answer is an emphatic "Yes." This may be the response that distinguishes you from other applicants and lands you the job.

- Can you work overtime?

Employers are legally allowed to require you to work overtime. More on whether they have to pay you extra in Chapter 6.

- Are you available for transfer to another location if the need arises?

Many companies have operations throughout the United States and overseas and are looking for employees who can readily transfer from one location to another during their career. In some companies, advancement depends on the ability to work in multiple locations.

- Can you use specific technologies, computer software or equipment? Can you use accounting, research, design or presentation tools? What is your level of skill in a specific area? Do you have any certificates or training beyond what is presented on your application?

It is legal for an employer to ask you to complete a specific job-related assignment, such as a presentation, spreadsheet or data analysis. The employer can ask you to complete the assignment at the interview or afterward.

- Are you available to entertain clients?

If you are applying for a job that is client facing, it is likely that spending time with clients at lunch, dinner, sporting or cultural events will be a key element of your job. Being comfortable with clients and ensuring that they feel valued and have a good time are important business skills.

● Do you have references?

Asking you to provide references is a perfectly legitimate interview question. But keep in mind that employers are not barred from contacting references other than those you provide.

● Do you intend to seek additional formal education?

If you're a college graduate and the interviewer asks you if you're going to get an MBA, the interview is not the moment for you to weigh the pros and cons of the degree.

● What did you accomplish on your last job?

This is your opportunity to advertise yourself and not practice false modesty. The key here is not simply to list your accomplishments on your last job, but to enumerate how these accomplishments relate to the job you're trying to obtain.

● Why did you leave your last job? What did you think of your former boss or coworkers? Were you ever fired?

Any time the interview touches on prior employment, you should emphasize how well you got along with your coworkers and your boss, and what you accomplished. You should avoid any badmouthing or complaining about prior work experiences. There is no way that such whining will reflect well on you, even if any past disagreements were not your fault.

Cameron was fired from her last job because she could not get along with her boss. The interviewer asks her directly, "Were you ever fired?" Cameron could say, "I worked for my former employer for five years and learned a lot. But in the end, I realized that it wasn't the right job for me, and decided that I wanted more challenging duties." Cameron does not have to admit that she was fired. Her response is still truthful and relevant to her new job opportunity

• What can you tell me about yourself? What are your hobbies?

The interviewer is trying to find out how you present yourself, how you talk extemporaneously about non-work topics, and whether you appear to have a chip on your shoulder or a negative attitude. Here, what you say matters much less than the manner in which you present your response.

• What are your career goals? Where do you see yourself in 5 years?

● What do you know about this company?

Before the interview, you should review publicly available information about the company, such as its website or annual report.

Conclusion

Interviews are important. You should know how to respond when interviewers ask questions about impermissible topics. Although there are legal remedies for being denied a job on the basis of race, age, sex, national origin, sexual orientation or disability, don't imagine that a lawsuit is a fruitful avenue to pursue. The best strategy is to make sure you receive a job offer.

2. OFFER LETTERS

Offer letters are extremely important. Sometimes you are so happy to have a job that you don't focus on the terms of the offer. It is crucial to remember that these terms will determine your compensation and benefits for a long time to come, and may control your employment options even after you leave the company.

In fact, your best bargaining position may be at the time of hire, when the employer is eager to fill the position. You might be able to negotiate a guaranteed future promotion or payment of a lost bonus from your previous job.

What is an offer letter

Most often, an employer will first offer you a job orally and then put the terms of the offer in writing. The written offer is called an offer letter. Offer letters can be printed or sent by email. The offer can be signed by an officer of the company or by a recruiter. Usually the company will request that you countersign the letter and return a copy by a specific date. If you do not sign and return the agreement by the specified time limit, the offer can be retracted.

It is essential that you keep a copy of the signed offer letter for your records. Frequently the offer letter refers to other documents, such as benefit plans or stock plans, that are posted on the employer's website. You need to download and keep copies of these supporting documents as well. Don't assume that these supporting documents will be electronically available when you're ready to leave. A company can amend a benefit or stock plan, but you may be bound by the versions in force when you were hired.

What are the most important elements of an offer letter

The most important elements of an offer letter are the following: the position for which you are being hired; your compensation; your benefits; your flexible work arrangements; your training; any preconditions to the offer; and what happens when you leave the company. More on each of these elements below.

If any of these items are not in the offer letter, you should inquire about them before accepting the job.

The position for which you are being hired

The first important element of the offer letter is a description of your job. That means more than just your job title. Here are the key components your need to look for.

• Your job title.

This should describe generally what you do, for example, Account Manager, Bookkeeper, Attorney, Systems Programmer.

• The level.

This refers to your position in the hierarchy of the company. For example, you could be an assistant vice president, a director, a senior vice president, a partner, or a "non-officer."

• The location.

Ideally you should know which building, campus or location you will work in. You definitely want to know the city where you will work.

• Whom you report to.

You may have more than one manager. That's not a problem in itself, but you should know this when you accept the offer.

Compensation

Compensation means more than just your salary. Here are the key components to look for.

• Your salary or hourly wage.

• Whether you're entitled to receive overtime pay.

More on who is eligible to overtime in Chapter 6.

• Your pay cycle.

Most commonly, you will be paid weekly, biweekly or monthly.

• Shift differential.

Some jobs require work outside the standard 9 a.m. to 5 p.m. schedule. Employers may pay an hourly premium for nontraditional work hours, such as a night shift.

• Sign-on bonus.

Sometimes the employer will give you a special payment upon joining the company. This payment is not tied to your wage or salary, or to your annual performance bonus. However, sometimes the offer letter will state that if you resign or are fired from the company within a certain period, you will have to return the special payment.

- Yearly bonus.

A yearly bonus can be paid in cash or stock. Even though the bonus may be awarded yearly, it can still be paid out to you in installments over time. Companies generally award annual bonuses on a specific date after the close of the year. For example, a company might award employee bonuses for the year 2014 on March 1, 2015. Your offer letter may indicate that you need to be employed on March 1 to receive your bonus for the prior year.

- Awards of company stock.

Stock can be granted in many forms. Deferred stock is stock to be granted in the future. Performance stock is based upon how well the company does financially. Options give you the ability to buy shares of stock at a fixed price, regardless of the current market price.

- Probationary period.

During a probationary period that generally lasts several months, the company may reserve the right to let you go for any reason, without going through the standard procedures for terminating an employee. However, the company cannot use this procedure to get around the laws against discrimination in firing.

● Performance review cycle.

You may get a raise or a bonus only at the end of a performance review cycle. You will need to know when these cycles end.

Benefits

Your non-wage benefits can add up to a significant fraction of your total compensation. Your decision to accept a job offer should depend on your total compensation, including benefits, and not just your wages.

● 401(k) plan.

In a 401(k) plan, you contribute part of your earnings into an account maintained by your employer. You don't pay income taxes on the money in this account while you're employed by the company. Some companies will match your contribution up to a predetermined limit. It is important that you contribute enough of your salary to take full advantage of your employer's matching contribution. It is free money that will otherwise disappear.

You can decide how to invest the money in your 401(k) account within limits set by your employer. While you're employed by the company, you may be able to borrow money from your 401(k) account for certain purposes, but this is generally a bad idea. If you leave the company for any reason, you will have to pay back the entire loan within a month or two, and if you don't repay the loan, you'll end up owing taxes and penalties.

• Traditional pension plan.

A traditional pension plan is money that is set aside by your employer for your retirement. It is not a 401(k) plan. Often you will not have any rights to this money until you have worked for the company for a minimum number of years.

• Deferred compensation plan.

Under a deferred compensation plan, you can contribute money to a separate account beyond what you can contribute to your 401(k) plan. These plans may be available to highly compensated employees.

• Health insurance, including dental and vision coverage.

Your offer letter may simply state whether you have health insurance coverage. You are well advised to contact the human resources department or the benefits representative of your company to learn the details. You'll want to know the monthly premium and deductibles, if any. You'll also want to know whether the health plan has restrictions, such as which doctors you can see or whether coverage of certain mental health services is limited.

Your company may also offer you a Medical Savings Account, which allows you to set aside money to pay healthcare expenses not covered by your insurance.

● Life insurance.

Your employer may provide life insurance coverage or offer you the option of purchasing life insurance.

● Short-term and long-term disability payments.

You may be entitled to partial salary payments if you are seriously ill and out of work for a certain amount of time.

● Vacation.

Your offer letter will state how many days of vacation you have each year. In general, the amount of vacation time increases as you continue to work for the company. You will also need to know whether any unused vacation days during one year can be carried over into the following year.

● Sick days.

Your offer letter will state how many days you can be out of work because of illness. You'll need to know whether unused sick days during one year can be carried over into the following year. You'll also need to know whether you'll be paid for any unused sick days if you leave the company.

- Other paid days off.

Sometimes employers will offer you paid days for volunteer work or other personal matters. These additional days do not count as vacation time or sick days.

Flexible work arrangements

Employers are permitted to establish any work schedule and location they want for their employees. Most companies have a set time to begin and end work, as well as fixed work locations. However, employees are sometimes permitted to set their own schedules or perform their duties outside regular worksites, including working from home. These are called flexible work arrangements.

You should know that employers are not legally required to provide flexible work arrangements for employees unless they are part of an accommodation for a disability. (More on disability accommodations in Chapter 8.) If you've decided to accept a job offer based on flexible hours or locations, you should be aware that your employer could revoke these arrangements at any time and for any reason. So you'll need to be prepared to make other changes in your life, if necessary.

Training and continuing education

Your offer letter may include tuition reimbursement for additional training or formal education.

Preconditions to the offer

Your offer letter will likely contain a provision that "this offer is contingent upon a satisfactory background investigation." Your offer may be withdrawn if you don't satisfy the company's standards in any of the following areas: criminal background check; credit check; education verification; employment check; immigration check; and reference verification. More on the details of background investigations in Chapter 3.

Your offer letter may ask you to certify that you are not bound by previous non-compete or non-solicitation agreements. If you are bound by such agreements, you need to inform your new employer. More on non-compete and non-solicitation agreements in Chapter 15.

You should be aware that the company can legally revoke its job offer if it identifies any misrepresentations in your application, even if they are minor. In fact, the company can terminate you even if it discovers such misrepresentations after you've already started the job.

Leaving the company

Finally, your offer letter may address what will happen when you leave the company.

• Severance and outplacement arrangements.

If you leave the company through no fault of your own, you might be eligible for severance payments to tide you over, as well as counseling services to help you find another job.

• References.

Your new employer may have a specific policy on what details of your employment it will be willing to share with future employers. More on employers' references in Chapters 12, 13 and 14, which address terminations.

• Limitations on your ability to work after you leave the company.

In return for offering you a job, your employer may require you to agree not to work for certain other companies or to solicit business from certain customers after you end your employment. More on non-compete agreements in Chapter 15.

Conclusion

Make sure you get all the important provisions of your job offer in writing. Oral promises will not be valuable when you leave the company. The manager who made them may have left. The manager may have forgotten. Or the manager may deny he ever made the promise.

3. BACKGROUND INVESTIGATIONS

Your job offer may be contingent upon a satisfactory background investigation.

You may be under the misimpression that an employer cannot delve into your personal background when you apply for a job. In fact, employers have legitimate, legal reasons to carry out background checks. They want to verify that you are who you say you are, and that you have done what you claim you have done. They want to protect their reputation from hiring someone who will bring negative publicity or ridicule upon the company. They may need to comply with certain federal and state laws that require background investigations in such industries as transportation, financial services, childcare and healthcare.

Big companies tend to use specialized investigatory agencies to perform background investigations. These agencies are legally required to inform the applicant under investigation at every step of the process. Companies who do their own background investigations have more flexibility.

Criminal records

Employers have to balance the safety and security of current employees against the fact that people with criminal records need to earn a living. Most states have limited the length of time an employer can consider a criminal record. The length of time depends on whether the past crime was a felony or a misdemeanor. Some states have required that the crime at issue be job related. Even if state law strictly limits what the employer can consider, there are overriding federal statutes and regulations in such fields as childcare, transportation and finance. At the end of the day, employers have had a lot of flexibility in looking for past evidence of violence, dishonesty and poor judgment.

The last few years have seen strong efforts to get employers to move away from strict time limits and instead to take a more holistic approach to criminal records. In response, the federal government has issued regulations that encourage employers to consider a number of factors beyond the mere fact that a crime was committed. These factors include: the nature of the crime; the length of time that has passed since the sentence was completed; the age of the perpetrator at the time of the crime; what has the perpetrator been doing since his sentence was completed; the nature of the job applied for; and any extenuating circumstances.

If you have been convicted of a crime, you need to figure out how to present your history in the best light possible.

> *A few years ago, Jake was present at a barroom brawl. When the police broke up the fight, they arrested every one in the immediate barroom area. Because Jake was visiting from out of town and did not have the resources to litigate the charge, his lawyer advised him to plead guilty to assault in return for probation. When Jake applies for a job, he is well advised to bring with him a dossier explaining the circumstances of the conviction. The dossier could include statements from his lawyer, statements from witnesses, and a copy of the police report that did not name him as one of the instigators.*

If you were convicted of a crime at a young age, the plea agreement may have included a provision that the conviction would be expunged from your criminal history so long as your record remained clean for a certain number of years. But when it comes time to apply for a job, don't count on it. Unfortunately, these supposedly expunged convictions are sometimes revealed by law enforcement agencies during a criminal background investigation. Although an employer is not supposed to consider such a conviction in your hiring decision, it is virtually impossible to prove that the employer indeed considered it.

If you have been convicted of a crime and your prospective employer asks for a criminal background check, you have the option of refusing. However, refusal to undergo a requested criminal background check is a guarantee that you will not be hired.

Employers are not permitted under any state or any federal law to disqualify applicants solely on the basis of arrests that have not led to a conviction. The only exception is a recent arrest whose disposition is still pending. In that case, the employer can postpone the hiring decision until the matter is resolved.

Credit check

Employers have two main reasons for performing credit checks. First, if an employee cannot manage his own finances, then it is less likely that he'll be able to work effectively on the job, where he'll need to have skills similar to budgeting money and paying bills on time. Second, if an employee has a record of bad debts, he may be more likely to steal from the company or engage in some form of dishonesty.

Employers have discretion in evaluating your credit history. It is unlikely that an employer would hold a late credit card payment against you. But if an overdue bill has gone to a collection agency or if a court has rendered a legal judgment on an overdue debt, then it is possible that these actions could bar your employment. Many employers look with great disfavor at tax liens or non-payment of taxes in any form. Others will disqualify you if you've defaulted on student loans. Most employers are more forgiving about debt due to medical bills, family emergencies or divorce. An applicant can be also penalized if there is no evidence of any credit use.

An employer who uses an outside agency must give you notice that your credit record is being checked and an opportunity to correct any errors. However, you will have only a limited amount of time to fix errors in your credit history, and your employer is not required to hold your job open in the meantime. Therefore, you should check your credit record and correct any errors before you apply. You can do so by requesting a free copy of your credit report from each of three credit agencies: Experian, TransUnion and Equifax. Each credit agency provides instructions as to how to request a correction.

Education, certification and licenses

With your consent, the employer can inquire about your educational background, including whether you have the degrees that you claim. Most companies will not hire you if you misrepresent your education. Even worse, they can terminate you if they later discover a discrepancy during your employment. It is entirely legal to do so. In fact, most employment applications state that any misrepresentation is grounds for termination.

Keep in mind that if you failed to pay your final college bill, it is likely that the college will claim you do not have a degree, even if you completed all the course work and even if you marched at graduation. If you state on your application that you already have an associate's or bachelor's degree because you anticipate receiving the degree in a few months, this would be considered a misrepresentation.

Most certifications and licenses are public records that can be verified. For many professions, your disciplinary history can be accessed as well. If you're the subject of a disciplinary action that is on the public record, you should make sure that your version of the facts is included in the record.

References

An employer can try to obtain references from your former employers. It can ask people whom you have not listed on your resume or your job application.

When asked about past employees, most employers will decline to give any information other than your dates of employment, your job title and your salary. That said, a bad reference could kill your chances of getting a job. Even if a company has a policy of no references, your future employer may find someone at your former company who will give a negative "off-the-record" reference. It will be almost impossible to determine if this happens, and there will be nothing you can do about it after the fact. If you're ambitious and want to advance from one company to another, don't make enemies.

An employer cannot say defamatory things about a former employee, but there is no law that prevents an employer from revealing factual information if it is true.

Drew was terminated from his previous job as an IT systems technician when it was learned that he had failed to back up any company records for three straight months. When Drew applied for another job, his former employer provided his dates of employment, job title and salary. However, in a phone call to the prospective employer, the old boss said that Drew was fired because his failure to carry out his job responsibilities caused significant harm to the business unit he supported. This off-the-

record reference may violate the company's policies on employee references, but it is not illegal.

Employers can also search the electronic trail of an applicant to look for antisocial behavior, biases, violence and other undesirable traits. Your electronic trail includes blogs, comments, tweets, "likes," as well as text, photo and video postings on such sites as Facebook, Vimeo, and Pinterest. It is a good idea to review your electronic history and, if possible, delete any questionable material. Unfortunately, posts that reflect badly on you may be controlled by others, who may not comply with your requests to erase them.

Military records

Employers can find out the name, rank, salary, duties, awards and duty status of a former military person but nothing beyond that. It is illegal for an employer to deny you a job because you might be called up to active duty.

Bankruptcy

Bankruptcy records are public, but an employer cannot refuse to hire you because you have filed for bankruptcy. Thus, an employer can hold your bad credit history against you, but once you file for bankruptcy, you do receive a level of protection against certain bad debts incurred prior to filing.

Driving records

Driving records are public. Employers have discretion in dealing with a record of drunk driving convictions. An employer can refuse to hire an applicant with any convictions. Another employer may determine that an applicant is disqualified only if he has two, three or four prior convictions.

Medical records

Medical records are not public and an employer cannot request or view them. The employer can ask the applicant if he can perform the essential functions of the job. If the applicant says that he can, the employer cannot require medical records to prove it. However, the employer can require that the applicant undergo a medical exam, provided that it requires the same medical exam of all applicants for similar jobs.

Katerina is applying for a position as a quality control inspector at a manufacturing company. The job requires inspections on numerous floors in several buildings throughout the workday. Katerina comes to the employment interview walking with a cane. Having described the position in detail, including its mobility requirements, the interviewer can legally ask Katerina whether she can perform the job. From the legal standpoint, Katerina is obligated only to respond yes or no. Nonetheless, if the answer is yes, it may be in Katerina's interest to explain that she had a prior job as an inspector where she successfully navigated a multisite manufacturing facility. Even if the interviewer has his doubts about Katerina's mobility, he cannot ask her for medical records to back up her conclusion.

Drug testing

Drug testing is legal. Drug testing generally screens for heroin, cocaine, marijuana, speed, Angel Dust, PCP, ketamine and other street drugs. Drug tests can be done by urine, blood, breath, saliva or hair analysis. Hair testing can detect drug use over a much longer time period.

Although some states require that drug tests for applicants be job related, in practice the employer has considerable leeway to decide what to screen for and whether a positive test is an automatic bar to employment at the time of the positive test, or even permanently.

If you are taking a drug with a doctor's prescription, such as oxycontin for pain or an amphetamine derivative for attention deficit, you will not be barred from employment by a positive drug test. But you will be asked to show your prescription.

You can be drug tested even if you are in a drug treatment program.

Conclusion

Take your background investigation very seriously. People with conditional job offers really do get disqualified because of something troubling in their background. It is crucial to understand all the aspects of a background investigation and to do your own review before you apply for jobs. Certain problems can be cleaned up easily. In other cases, you'll need to be prepared to put the best light on an unfortunate incident in the past.

4. MENTORING

Mentoring can be an invaluable tool in your success at a company, and it can help you advance in your career. You want to be able to take full advantage of the relationship with your mentor, seeking his counsel and experience. Whether your relationship is formal or informal, you need to know the rules of mentoring so that you do not cross the line into inappropriate behavior.

What is mentoring

Mentoring is a voluntary relationship in which a mentor provides advice, help, encouragement or support to a mentee. Usually the mentor is a more senior person in your organization, but not necessarily so. It can be someone in another department, someone with a different skill set, someone who has a different support network or someone with a different perspective.

There are two ways you can get a mentor. In a large company with a formal mentoring program, you will be assigned a mentor. If there is no formal mentoring program, it will be your responsibility to approach someone who you think would be an appropriate mentor for you.

The value of having a mentor

• When you are new to a company, a mentor can acclimate you to your job.

Joseph's manager was responsible for enumerating his duties and prioritizing them. But Joseph looked to his mentor for tips on who in the company knows what, who could be a valuable resource and who should be avoided.

• A mentor can transmit unwritten rules and norms of a company.

Part of Ian's job involved entertaining wealthy clients. Although his company had a general travel and entertainment policy, it did not explicitly spell out how much Ian could spend on lunches, dinners or other events. Ian's mentor helped him create a budget, plan events within that budget, and satisfy his wealthy clients without violating the company's unwritten norms.

- A mentor can help you advance.

Midori works for a company that does not have a formal system for promotions. Instead, employees get promoted when they impress senior managers with their work on projects that come to the managers' attention. Midori's mentor suggested a number of projects for her to work on, emphasized the importance of doing well and strategized with her on how to present the project results to senior management.

- A mentor can empower you to take responsibility for your actions by providing psychological support.

In the company's tax department, tight deadlines required that Ashleigh work twenty days straight without a day off. At points during these marathon work sessions, Ashleigh had the urge to yell at her manager or at a coworker who made an error that caused her to work even later. At these times, Ashleigh was able to make a quick detour to her mentor's office, blow off steam to a sympathetic ear and return to her work effectively.

- A mentor can help you plan your career.

Vincent started with the company at an entry-level position. He thought the only way to advance was to stay in his current department and continue to be promoted up the job ladder. Vincent's mentor explained that the company actually valued mastering more than one discipline in different departments before granting promotions. His mentor encouraged him to make strategic lateral moves that ultimately enabled Vincent to move up the corporate hierarchy.

- A mentor can introduce you to new people and help you network.

  Adriana works in government relations, but aspires to work in the company's in-house charitable foundation. Adriana's mentor invited her to several charitable events where she met executives committed to helping the community in which the company was headquartered. When an opening came up in the foundation, Adriana contacted the executives she had met at the charitable events and asked for their support of her job application.

- A mentor can serve as a role model.

  Alan's mentor had a high-level, high-pressure position, but always acted respectfully to his peers and his subordinates. Alan realized how difficult it was not to take your frustrations out on others, and aspired to emulate his mentor's behavior.

The mentee's obligations

As a mentee, you need to stay open minded. Listen, consider, and don't cling to preconceived ideas about the way to function in the workplace. You need to commit to change and growth. You're not just going to pass the time sitting in your mentor's office. At the same time, you need to be realistic about your career and what you want. Mentoring is not pie in the sky. It's grounded in reality. Ultimately, you have to understand that the mentoring relationship is a resource, not a mandate. It is your obligation to consider the recommendations of your mentor, but always to act in accord with your own values.

Rules

There are no laws governing the mentor relationship and a company may not have a formal mentoring program. If a company does have a formal mentoring program, it will establish rules governing the mentor-mentee relationship. These include the amount of time the mentor is willing to commit, the eligibility criteria for serving as a mentor, and whether any corporate resources are available to support the mentoring relationship.

Why people want to be mentors

While it might seem that accomplished executives would have no interest in serving as mentors, in fact many do. They want to pass on what they have learned. They get personal satisfaction helping others. They want to expand their own network and their understanding of other parts of the organization.

A mentee needs to be alert to danger signs that the relationship is not working

Not all mentoring relationships work. Here are some of the danger signs to look for. Your mentor may be too controlling. Your mentor may violate your confidentiality. Or your mentor may try to intervene directly in a work problem that you're having.

Mentor relationships are voluntary from both perspectives. Either the mentor or mentee can end the relationship at any time. If you notice any of the danger signs, it may be time for you to end the relationship.

Lines that the mentee should not cross

A mentee should never use a meeting with his mentor as therapy for his personal problems. You can discuss your interpersonal problems with coworkers, but this is not the place to discuss what went on last night with your spouse. A mentee should not breach the confidentiality of the mentor-mentee relationship. What the mentor tells you is not to be repeated. A mentee should not drop his mentor's name in order to intimidate others. Don't tell the IT staff that your computer problem needs instant attention because your mentor demands it. In the same vein, a mentee should not undermine his manager by quoting his mentor.

Conclusion

When highly successful people talk about their careers, they often mention the role that a mentor played. Since it is hard to be realistic all the time about your abilities, goals, work needs and work relationships, a mentor or trusted advisor can be invaluable. The key is to get matched with the right one and take appropriate advantage of the relationship.

5. PERFORMANCE EVALUATIONS

It is quite stressful to have someone else evaluate your performance on the job. That said, you can turn your annual performance evaluation into a valuable tool. You need to prepare for your review. You should be able to detail the positive contributions you have made. If your manager identifies areas for improvement, you need to approach the evaluation with an open mind. Whether your evaluation is written or oral or both, by the end of the critique you should have a clear road map of what needs to be done to improve your performance.

Why do employers do performance evaluations

Employers want to make sure that the work of the company gets done in an accurate and timely manner. To that end, they create descriptions for each job, along with a listing of the job's goals and objectives. Your performance on your job is measured against these goals and objectives.

No law requires employers to give performance evaluations. But if your employer decides to evaluate your performance, the process must not consider your age, gender, race, national origin, sexual orientation, religion or disability.

Managers use performance evaluations to motivate and reward you. The evaluation is the basis for determining if you need further training or discipline. If your work is unsatisfactory, it can be the basis for your termination.

Pinning down your goals and objectives

It is your responsibility to review and understand the goals and objectives of your job. You can't do better if you don't know what you're supposed to be better at. You can't do better if you don't know how. Your job goals need to be understandable, measurable, attainable and consistent with the objectives of your department and company.

Amy has been a public relations officer at the company for two years. She has just gone through her second performance evaluation. At the start of the meeting, her manager commented that she met all of her deadlines and her written communications accurately transmitted the message that the company wanted to convey. However, her manager mentioned several times during the meeting that Amy was still viewed as "green." As a result, the company was reluctant to assign her to work on high-profile projects. At the close of the meeting, Amy's manager reiterated that he was very happy with her performance and that she had acclimated well to her job. Amy left the evaluation with a smile, but she failed to clear up an absolutely critical point -- namely, what it means to be "green" and what she needs to do in the coming year to get assigned to more important assignments. If Amy later realizes that she has not pinned down this critical aspect of her job goals, she should schedule a follow-up meeting with her manager. There is nothing improper about this. Requesting such a meeting will not make Amy look weak or insecure.

Your evaluation may focus on your immediate past performance, but you need to look beyond that into the future. You need to stretch yourself, to set higher goals, to learn new skills that will add value to the company. This is not simply a matter of more training. You need to build a support network of people who will help you in the future. You need to network with people who will give you new opportunities.

How you will be evaluated

Before your manager begins your evaluation, he will generally look at your job description, goals, compensation history, prior evaluations and any disciplinary warnings. If you're concerned that your manager does not have an important piece of information, such as a favorable customer satisfaction survey, you should provide this information to your manager before or during the evaluation.

Your manager will base your evaluation not just on his own experience with you. He will often seek input from clients, coworkers, your subordinates and other managers.

Your manager will look not only at the quality, accuracy and timeliness of your work, but also at your teamwork, leadership, independence, flexibility, initiative and your compliance with the company's ethics.

Cyrus never missed a deadline. He had the highest ratings on all customer satisfaction surveys. But everyone knew that Cyrus did not like people from India and that Cyrus did not want the company's new recruits from India servicing any of his customers. Also, Cyrus had come to feel so comfortable with his customers that he often told them raunchy jokes in phone conversations that could be heard by everyone in the area. Finally, when Cyrus completed his individual assignments for the day, rather than working on departmental projects, he would use the company's computer to monitor orders for his personal side business delivering flowers. Cyrus used the company's photocopier to reproduce fliers for his business. When it came time for Cyrus' performance evaluation, he expected the highest rating and a big raise. He was taken aback when the entire evaluation focused on his racism, his inappropriate comments to customers and his misuse of corporate resources.

Two factors can complicate the evaluation process: working at a location far from your manager; and having more than one manager. If a significant geographic distance separates you from your manager, you will need to work extra hard to make sure he knows what you've been doing and to convince him that your work is valuable to the company. You don't want to be evaluated by a stranger. If you have more than one manager, you may find yourself with conflicting goals and recommendations. Before your evaluation, you need to figure out how to present your accomplishments in a way that satisfies both managers.

Monique has two different managers, both of whom are senior executives in product development. Over the course of the year, each one of them wanted Monique to work solely on his project. This put Monique in the unenviable position of having constantly to stop work on one project to work on the other one, leaving both managers frustrated with her. Monique tried to get a department head to mediate between the two supervisors, but that didn't work. When it came time for her performance review, Monique risked getting bad evaluations from both of her superiors. Monique's best strategy is to come to her evaluation prepared to show in detail how much work she did for both managers. Monique needs to send the message that she has actually excelled at two full-time assignments, rather than muddling through two half-time jobs.

Traps that managers fall into

Managers are human. Their evaluations are not always fair and balanced. You can be guaranteed that at some point in your career, a manager will jump to incorrect conclusions about your performance based on faulty reasoning. To protect your record, you need to understand the most common logical traps that managers fall into.

Rather than evaluating your performance throughout the entire evaluation period, a manager may focus inappropriately on a single incident because it was negative or occurred quite recently.

A key part of Cindy's job was giving weekly presentations to the company's clients on current market conditions. During the year, 51 of Cindy's presentations were flawless. The materials were delivered in advance to clients, who were also able to follow the slides that she projected on the screen. On the day of the last presentation, Cindy's computer died. She could not email mate-

rials to clients in advance, and her slide presentation was buried in her nonfunctional hard disc. During Cindy's performance review, her manager did not mention any of the research that went into any of Cindy's presentations during the year. Nor did her manager note that Cindy had given 51 flawless presentations. Instead, the manager explained that he was giving Cindy a low rating because last week, her presentation appeared to be disorganized and the clients seemed to be confused. When Cindy tried to put the mishap of the final presentation in context, her manager got angry. In this situation the only thing that Cindy can do is to present her accomplishments in a factual and professional manner in the employee comment section of the evaluation.

Some managers tend to reward people whom they see as clones of themselves. They tend to reward subordinates who solve problems in exactly the same way they would have, even if there are other ways to get the job done.

Susan's job was to install phones for new employees and explain to them how the phone system worked. Her manager Hugh had performed Susan's job before he was promoted. When Hugh made his rounds, he would regularly engage in small talk with the employees along his route. Susan, on the other hand, simply installed the phones, gave the necessary training and left her pager number. In fact, because Susan did not socialize at every workstation along the way, her productivi-

ty was 25% higher than Hugh's productivity was. When Hugh gave Susan her performance evaluation, he focused on what he perceived as her robotic and cold demeanor in the performance of her duties. Hugh agreed that no one had complained about Susan and that, quite the contrary, people were very happy with her service. Yet Hugh continued to insist that backslapping is a crucial part of the job, and he gave Susan a low performance rating. Susan is well advised to seek a lateral transfer to another manager.

Conclusion

Your performance review is just like any other job assignment. You can't just show up without any preparation. You should make sure that you've done everything possible to document your accomplishments and present them in the best possible light. You may have the opportunity to fill out a self-evaluation form, but if you don't, you'll need to create your own form.

A short, vague positive review is almost as bad as a negative review. If your manager indeed believes that you are a valued employee with a future at the company, you want to give him the tools to produce a positive, useful and thoughtful review.

6. OVERTIME PAY

The legal basis for overtime pay is a federal law called the Fair Labor Standards Act (or FLSA). Each state has its own regulations on overtime pay, but the main concepts are the same as in the federal law.

Under the FLSA, employees are entitled to be paid for every hour they work. Moreover, they are entitled to be paid time-and-one-half of their hourly rate for all hours worked over forty during each workweek.

Employees covered by these rules are called "nonexempt employees." If you are a nonexempt employee, it will say so in your offer letter, in your personnel file and sometimes on your pay stub.

On the other hand, if your company specifically identifies you as a manager, administrator or professional, then you are an "exempt" employee and you are not entitled to overtime pay. This determination does not depend on your job title, but on the nature of your work, your responsibilities and your salary level. The precise rules are very strict and are spelled out in the FLSA.

If you are a nonexempt employee, this chapter is for you.

Companies can require employees to work overtime

Your employer can make you work as much overtime as it wants. There is no legal limit on the amount of time an employer can require you to work, so long as you are paid time-and-one-half for your overtime hours. Your employer does not have to give you advance notice before ordering you to work overtime.

Bethany, a nonexempt employee, regularly works from 8 a.m. to 4 p.m. Because her department was short staffed that day, the required work was not finished by 4 p.m. Without notice, her manager told Bethany to stay and complete the remaining tasks. Bethany might try to negotiate with her manager to see if someone else could stay late. But the bottom line is that if Bethany refuses, she runs the risk of being fired.

Hourly rate

Every nonexempt job has an hourly rate and by law it must be higher than the federal minimum wage and the specific state minimum wage. For each hour worked over 40 hours, you must receive overtime pay at the rate of 1.5 your regular rate of pay. Each workweek stands alone for purposes of computing overtime pay. The standard workweek starts at 12:00 a.m. on Monday and ends at 11:59 p.m. Sunday.

Your employer cannot swap hours between workweeks to avoid paying you overtime. Your employer cannot pressure you into waiving your overtime pay.

Stephen is being interviewed for an entry-level job in the company. The interviewer tells Stephen that there are dozens of applicants for the job and that he is looking for an applicant who won't charge the company for overtime hours. Stephen desperately wants the job and feels pressured to agree to forego his overtime pay. The deal proposed by the interviewer is illegal. If Stephen takes the job and works overtime, he has to be paid for it.

Tina has several small children, so time off during the afternoon is extremely valuable to her. Tina just worked 50 hours a week for two weeks in a row. Her manager offers her five free afternoons during the coming week if she forgoes the overtime pay for the past two weeks. Even though both Tina and her manager would like to make such a deal, it is illegal. The manager can give Tina as much time off with pay as he wants, but he has to pay her time-and-one-half for the 20 hours of overtime she just worked.

What counts as hours worked

The location of the work does not determine whether it is compensable. Work can be performed at the home, at a client's place of business or on the road.

Work done on a regular telephone, smart phone, tablet or computer counts as work. Allowed break time counts as work time. Training time can count as work if attendance is mandatory and if it the training is job related.

On-call time may count as hours worked. On the other hand, if you can carry out your regular activities with minimal interruption while you're on call, then it doesn't count as hours worked. The regulations issued under the FLSA consider four factors: how quickly you must respond to a call or inquiry; how often you're interrupted while you're on call; how far you'd have to travel to perform the task or take care of the problem; and whether you're the only employee on call.

When Greg is on call over the weekend, he gets an average of 12 email inquiries, each of which he can respond to within 5 minutes. Greg does not have to leave his home. He can respond to the emails no matter where he is. Although Greg is the only person on call, he would not be paid for the entire weekend.

Greg would be paid only for the hour he spent on average re-
sponding to emails.

Attendance at outside events that are work related can count as work time. For example, attendance at diversity events, store openings, sporting events, dedications and award dinners may be work time if these events are sponsored or encouraged by the company.

Travel time from your home to workplace and back is not work time. However, travel time from one work site to another during the day is work time. Travel time during a business trip is more complicated. As a general rule, business travel during your regular work time counts as work hours, even if you travel on the weekends. Travel after hours does not.

Management must pay for all work even if it isn't authorized

Management can require that you get permission to work overtime. If you don't get permission and work overtime anyway, you could be disciplined or even fired, but you must still be paid. To avoid this pitfall, you're well advised to pin down what tasks your manager wants you to complete within what time frame.

Inez is under financial strain. She could get her assignments
done during an 8-hour workday, but she intentionally dawdles
until 5 p.m. so that she can then earn three additional hours of

overtime. Joel would like nothing better than to finish his work by 5 p.m., but he is so inefficient that he ends up working until 8 p.m. In both cases, Inez and Joel have earned overtime pay, but their employers are well within their rights to instruct them that the work must be completed by 5 p.m. If they continue to work until 8 p.m., they can be fired.

Justin and Claudia worked in the kitchen at a chain restaurant. Justin finished his normal shift at 5 p.m. Claudia was supposed to continue to work through 10 p.m., but had to leave early for personal reasons. Justin covered for Claudia from 5 to 10 p.m. without asking permission to do so. While Justin was well advised to clear the time swap with his manager, he still merits overtime pay. Claudia will not be paid for the time she missed.

Brian was scheduled for a lunch break from 12 to 1 p.m., but there were customers still waiting to be served. So Brian worked the entire lunch period. Brian's manager refused to pay him because that was not a scheduled work hour and his manager hadn't budgeted for it. In fact, Brian is owed pay for the additional hour worked. The company's written procedures required that employees could not leave the premises if there were still customers in the queue. What's more, Brian's manager was in a nearby glass-enclosed office and could clearly see that Brian was working.

What doesn't count as hours worked

Time spent on the premises that is unrelated to your job does not count as time worked. If you come into work before your designated start time to have breakfast in the company cafeteria or type your term paper for night school, your time spent on these activities does not count as hours worked.

Those days that you spend out of the office for vacation, illness, holidays, bereavement and jury duty do not count as hours worked.

What's included in computing the hourly rate

You need to know your hourly rate in order to compute your overtime rate. Not only does your regular pay count, but also your shift differential and your bonus for good performance. More on shift differentials in Chapter 2.

The monetary value of holiday gifts, special achievement awards, profit sharing, awards for long-term service and reimbursement for expenses do not count in computing your hourly rate.

Record keeping

An employer is obligated to maintain a record of hours worked for every nonexempt employee. The employer can use a time clock, or it can ask employees to maintain their own records and submit them at the end of the week.

If you intentionally misrepresent the hours that you worked, it can be considered both fraud and theft of company property, and it can be grounds for termination. If you claim overtime pay for hours that you didn't work, your employer can sue you for repayment, and it can also report you to law enforcement authorities for theft.

If you complain to the government that you have not been paid overtime and it turns out that your employer has not maintained a record of your hours worked, then the government can presume that your own records of hours worked are correct.

Conclusion

Managers are under constant pressure to get the work done within their budget. When the workload exceeds the budget, your manager may try to pressure you to work additional hours without recording overtime. Especially in times of layoffs, reductions in force and limited job opportunities, you may feel that you have to cave in. If you do, you're being cheated out of money that is legally yours. A better approach is to work with your manager to prioritize your responsibilities during the usual 40-hour workweek and to receive authorization to work overtime if absolutely necessary.

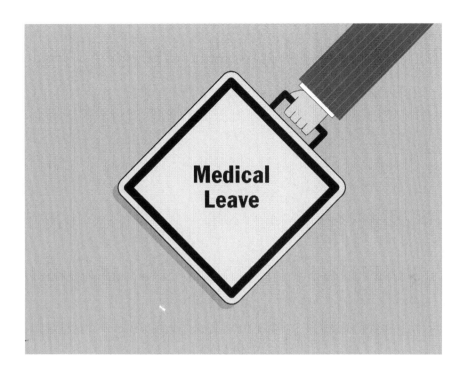

7. FAMILY MEDICAL LEAVE ACT

You are entitled to take time off from work for your own illness or an illness of a close family member. The Family Medical Leave Act (FMLA) does not require that you be paid for the time off, but it prohibits your employer from terminating you for these absences.

Who is eligible

You are eligible for this job-protected leave if you have worked for your employer for twelve months (which need not be consecutive) and for at least 1,250 hours during the 12-month period prior to the start of your leave. In addition, you must be working at a location where at least 50 people are employed. There are a few industries with fluctuating workweeks, such as airlines and public safety, that have different eligibility criteria.

The amount of protected leave

You are eligible for twelve weeks of leave each year. Your employer can choose whether to use a calendar year or a fiscal year in calculating the amount of your leave.

> *Gemma's mother fell at home and broke her left hip. Gemma took an 8-week leave to care for her after she was discharged from the rehabilitation center. Unfortunately, six months later, Gemma's mother fell again and broke her right hip. It appears that Gemma's mother will need another 8 weeks of help. Gemma's FMLA leave is still limited to a total of 12 weeks during the year, even if her mother can't get out of the bed to go to the bathroom. Quite apart from the law, Gemma might be allowed to take an additional unpaid leave or to use up her vacation time, but only at the discretion of her manager.*

Pay and insurance during the leave

The FMLA only requires that your employer give you a medical leave. It does not require that your employer pay you during the leave. However, your employer may allow you or even require you to use your accrued sick pay or vacation pay for some part of the FMLA leave. During your FMLA leave, your employer cannot discontinue your health insurance.

When you return from your leave, you must receive any regular bonus you would otherwise have received, unless your bonus depended on specific assignments that you did not complete.

What justifies the leave

You can take an FMLA leave for the birth of a child and the care of a newborn, for adoption or foster care, for your own serious health condition, or for the care of a spouse, child or parent with a serious health condition. The Act has strict rules about which close family members are covered. For example, a parent can be a step, foster, adoptive or biological parent or someone who raised you in the role of a parent, but it does not count in-laws. However, your company may be more lenient, and it is worth inquiring. The Act has special rules for caring for members of the military.

Natalia had already used up all of her regular sick days. Unfortunately, her dental crown came off while she was eating hard candy. As a result, Natalia had to miss two more days of work, initially to have the dentist give her a temporary crown and then to replace it with a permanent crown. Natalia applied for two days of leave under the FMLA. Her employer could legally deny her FMLA leave as a non-serious condition and fire her for unsatisfactory attendance.

Sergio's dog Chesterfield was dying from leukemia. Sergio spent four days at the veterinary hospital, helping to care for Chesterfield until he finally passed away. Sergio asked for FMLA leave because his dog was hospitalized with a critical illness and because he had lavished as much care and attention on Chesterfield as he would on his own son. With legal justification, Sergio's employer denied his request. (Sergio's request for bereavement leave was also denied.)

Intermittent versus continuous leave

You can take an FMLA leave for one continuous time period or your leave can be broken up into multiple time periods. The latter is called intermittent FMLA leave. In the case of continuous leave, the maximum duration is 12 weeks each year. In the case of intermittent leave, the limit is still 12 weeks, but the total time can be spread out over the entire year.

If you have a baby or adopt a child, you can take a leave at any time during the first year after birth or placement, but your leave must be continuous. If you need intermittent leave for a newborn or adopted child, you need your company's permission.

If you and your spouse are both employed at the same company, then the two of you only receive 12 weeks combined to care for a newborn, adopted child or a seriously ill parent. However, if you and your spouse both have serious illnesses, each of you is entitled to 12 weeks of leave.

Intermittent leave can be taken when medically necessary to care for a seriously ill family member or yourself. But you have an obligation to try to schedule an intermittent leave in a way that minimizes the adverse effect on the company.

Amber suffers from post-traumatic stress disorder. As part of her therapy, she needs to see a psychologist for a one-hour session once each week. Amber may take intermittent leave to see her therapist, but she has an obligation to try to schedule the sessions at the least disruptive time during the workweek, such as Friday at 4 p.m. or in the early morning.

What serious medical conditions justify a leave

Your medical problem will qualify as a serious condition if you are under a doctor's care for more than three days, if you are in the hospital, if you're pregnant or have a prenatal medical problem, or if you need treatments such as chemotherapy or physical therapy. You also qualify if you have a chronic illness that requires at least biannual visits to a healthcare provider over an extended length of time and that may cause episodic rather than continuing bouts of incapacity. The same criteria apply to the illness of a close family member.

What the company can and cannot do

During an intermittent leave, your employer can move you to a less disruptive position if your leave interferes with your company's ability to get the work done. When your leave is completed, whether it is intermittent or continuous, your employer must assign you to your original job or to a similar job with same pay, benefits and other terms of employment.

Your employer can require a doctor's certificate stating your medical diagnosis and the reason you need to be out of work. If the doctor's certificate is incomplete, your employer can ask for more information. If your company doubts the validity of the doctor's opinion, it can require a second medical opinion. Your company can also request that the doctor's certification be renewed periodically. Finally, your employer can require a fitness-for-duty certificate before you return to work. Beyond these certifications, your employer cannot compel you to submit your underlying medical records.

Chris suffers from asthma. His severe asthma attacks have been occurring about five times per month, but it is impossible to predict when they will occur. Chris applies for 12 weeks of intermittent family medical leave spread out over one year. His medical condition is supported by his doctor's certification. His employer grants his leave with two conditions. First, he must submit a confirmation from his doctor every three months stat-

ing that his medical condition still requires the leave. Second, during his leave, Chris will transfer from his job in portfolio management, which has daily deadlines, to a job in the research department, which does not have daily deadlines.

Conclusion

The FMLA is an extremely valuable benefit for employees. Most people will have a serious illness or need to care for a close family member with a serious illness at least once during the course of their employment. The FMLA prevents you from losing your job when this happens. It is important to understand what the Act covers and what it does not cover, so that you request what you're legally entitled to receive. And it is just as important that you understand the medical certification requirements, so that your leave is not denied after you've already been away from your job for some time.

8. DISABILITIES

If you already have a disability when you're hired, or if you become disabled during the course of your employment, it is essential that you know your rights.

The main source of protection for applicants and employees with disabilities is a far-reaching federal law called the Americans with Disabilities Act (ADA). Most states have additional protections for disabled people, but state laws generally adhere to the concepts of the federal law.

Which employers are covered by the ADA

The ADA covers private employers, as well as state and local governments, so long as they have 15 or more employees.

What aspects of employment are covered

The ADA covers all aspects of employment, including job applications, attendance policies, compensation, employee meetings, job training, performance evaluations, promotions and terminations.

Elena has a vision disability. She has to sit in the front row during all meetings and presentations. Her manager hastily announces a department meeting to discuss a new project. Elena is one of the last people to arrive. Elena's manager has an obligation under the ADA to ask someone in the first row to give up his seat so that Elena can see the screen.

Who is considered disabled under the law and thus entitled to protection

As a job applicant or employee, you are considered disabled if you have a physical or mental impairment that substantially limits one or more major life activities. The law also applies if you have a record of such an impairment or if you are regarded as having such an impairment.

Kit has been in remission from early-stage Hodgkin's lymphoma for five years. She's applying for a position that requires building extensive relationships with clients over an extended period. The recruiter does not want to hire her. He fears that if Kit has a relapse of cancer in two years, all of the groundwork of getting to know the company's key clients will be wasted. Kit is perfectly capable of performing her job duties. Kit is protected under the ADA because she has a record of an impairment. Refusing to hire Kit because she might have a relapse is illegal under the Act.

What impairments entitle you to protection

You are entitled to protection if your impairment substantially limits one or more major life activities. A major life activity includes caring for yourself, seeing, hearing, eating, sleeping, walking, standing, sitting, reaching, lifting, bending, speaking, breathing, learning, reading, concentrating and interacting with others.

The list of specific impairments is extensive. It includes deafness, blindness, missing limbs, autism, cancer, diabetes, epilepsy, HIV infection, multiple sclerosis, depression, post-traumatic stress disorder, obsessive-compulsive disorder, attention deficit disorder and schizophrenia. In general, such conditions as old age, poverty, seasonal allergies, self-limited colds and flu, and uncomplicated sprains and fractures are not considered disabilities under the ADA. Various sexual disorders such as pedophilia, as well as compulsive gambling, klepto-mania and pyromania are not covered.

Symptoms, traits and behaviors are not mental disabil-ities in themselves. Some examples are: being stressed; being chronically late for work; missing deadlines; exer-cising poor judgment at work or in your personal life; being unfriendly; failing to get enough sleep or having difficulty falling asleep; failing to take medicine as pre-scribed; and exhibiting signs of racism or sexism.

> *Warren was accused of sexual harassment. He admitted repeat-edly fondling and caressing his administrative assistant. When informed that he would be terminated for this behavior, Warren claimed that he had poor impulse control and requested an ac-commodation for this disability under the ADA. Warren's request for protection would be denied for two reasons. First, be-ing unable to prevent yourself from touching other employees is not a disability. Second, a request for accommodation must come before the employee violates a workplace standard.*

Even if you are not disabled, the ADA will protect you against discrimination if you have a relationship with someone who has a disability.

> *A promotion has opened up in Teresa's department at work. Teresa's husband has multiple sclerosis. Her manager assumes that she will be frequently out of work to care for him and thus gives the promotion to a less qualified peer. Her manager's ac-tion violates the ADA, which protects Teresa against*

discrimination. Teresa is not entitled to special treatment or affirmative action, but cannot be disadvantaged solely on the speculation that she would be frequently out of work.

Reasonable accommodation

To be entitled to protection under the ADA, you must be able to perform the essential functions of your job with or without reasonable accommodation. The essential functions of the job are its most important duties. They are the reason the job exists at all. Reasonable accommodation is a change in the usual way that the job is performed.

Reasonable accommodation includes physical changes in the work space, including desks, chairs, computers or other equipment, or connecting stairs or ramps. It also includes changes in job schedules or duties. Reasonable accommodation applies not only to the performance of the job, but also to applying for the job, to testing for job eligibility and to on-the-job training.

Deborah works as an executive assistant to a senior vice president. She performs all the essential functions of the job, including typing, calendar management, travel arrangements, ordering supplies and answering the phones. Because Deborah uses a wheelchair, she cannot reach the supplies that are stored in overhead cabinets. Her manager is obligated to accommodate her impairment. In fact, he has arranged with another employee to determine twice weekly what supplies Deborah needs and place them on her desk. Reaching for the supplies is not an essential function of Deborah's job, and having another employee spend a few minutes each week accessing the supplies is not unreasonable.

Michael has a sleep disorder. Even with medication, he cannot fall asleep before 2 a.m. and does not wake up until 10 a.m. Michael has requested an accommodation that permits him to work from 11 a.m. to 7 p.m. Because Michael works in the project management office, he has to submit a report on the final Friday of every month, but he has no daily deadlines. The building is regularly open until 10 p.m. and Michael does not need to rely on the presence of coworkers to get his work done. Michael's manager would be obligated to accept this accommodation in work schedule.

Reasonable accommodation can include reassigning you to another position if one is available. But your employer does not have to create a special or "make work" job for you. The ADA does not require your employer to bump another employee out of his job to make room for you even if you're disabled and are qualified for the job.

Zachary suffers from claustrophobia. He is prone to having panic attacks when he is in enclosed spaces. He currently works as a customer service representative in a call center, where the work area is divided into small cubicles. The floor below houses data analysts, who work in a wide-open space with no dividers between workstations. As an accommodation, Zachary requests *reassignment to a data analyst position. Unfortunately, there are no openings for a data analyst. Zachary's company would not be required to remove one of the current data analysts and put Zachary in his place.*

An employer must make a reasonable accommodation unless doing so would cause an undue hardship. An undue hardship would involve significant difficulty or expense. A profitable company will find it hard to prove that an accommodation would cause an undue hardship.

A change in the parking rules can be a reasonable accommodation if you have mobility limitations that make it difficult to walk from a distant parking lot. But transportation to and from your job will remain your responsibility.

Allowing a service dog to come to work can be a reasonable accommodation. But it will be your responsibility to acquire the dog. The same applies to other personal items, such as a wheelchair, special lenses or a hearing aid.

Requesting an accommodation

If you have a disability, it's your responsibility to ask for a reasonable accommodation. Your employer is not obligated to discover your disability.

When you request an accommodation, you don't have to refer specifically to the ADA or use the legal term "reasonable accommodation." You can request an accommodation at any time during the course of your employment.

Once you request a reasonable accommodation, you and your manager will work out whether there is a solution that will keep you on the job. Ordinarily, you would propose a specific change. Your manager is not required to accept your initial proposal. If your manager believes that your proposal will be too expensive or unreasonably interfere with the work of the company, he can offer alternatives. If your employer offers a reasonable solution that would allow you to perform your job, and if you then refuse to accept it, you could be terminated.

For 15 years, Constantine was able to perform his job as a financial analyst. Four years ago, his vision began to deteriorate and he needed an adjustment in the font sizes of his computer monitor. Now Constantine has requested an expensive 32-inch monitor screen. His manager has proposed less expensive screen magnification software. Constantine agrees to try out the screen magnification software, which in fact permits him to continue to do his work.

Anna is hearing impaired. She has been able to perform all the essential duties of her job using a special telecommunications device called a TTD. Her company just went through a merger and all employees in Anna's group must undergo training in a new software program. The day before the training session, Anna asks her manager to provide a sign language interpreter.

Despite the manager's efforts, it is impossible to get an interpreter at such short notice. Her manager proposes several alternatives. He can have another employee take notes for her. Or she can take a one-month unpaid leave until the next training session, at which time a sign language interpreter will be available. Anna rejects both alternatives because she has had unfortunate experiences with others taking notes for her and because she feels it's unfair to lose a month's pay when it was not her fault. Since Anna can't perform the essential functions of the job without training in the new software and since she has rejected two reasonable alternative accommodations, she could be fired.

Applying for a job

When you apply for a job, the interviewer is not allowed ask to you whether you have a disability. He cannot ask you, "How's your health?" or "Have you been sick lately?" Nor can he ask questions about the symptoms or prognosis of a specific condition. The interviewer can only ask you whether you can perform the essential functions of the job.

Dorothy has an EMT certification. She applies to work as a medic for a company that provides patient transport services. Dorothy can be asked whether she is able to carry a patient on a stretcher along with another medic. She cannot be asked whether she has any back problems, whether she has any old sports injuries or how much she herself weighs.

More on interviewing and job applications in Chapter 1.

Drug and alcohol use

If you currently use illegal drugs, you are not protected under the ADA, even if you have a disability. If you are a job applicant or an employee, you can be tested for illegal drugs. Alcoholism is considered an impairment under the ADA. However, your employer can terminate you if you're drinking on the job or if your drinking off the job interferes with your job performance.

Bruce is an alcoholic. He continues to attend mandatory AA meetings weekly. The only AA meeting in his area takes place on Thursday afternoons. Unless an essential job duty has to be performed at that time, Bruce's employer must accommodate his need to attend. However, if Bruce starts drinking again to the extent that it affects his attendance, he can be fired.

Violent or threatening conduct

An employer may establish standards of behavior in order to protect its employees from harm. If you violate these standards, your employer can fire you even if the violation is a consequence of your disability. In deciding whether to fire you because you're dangerous, your employer has to identify specific violent or threatening behaviors. It's not enough to assume that a certain condition will result in violent or threatening conduct.

In a moment of indiscretion, David disclosed to his manager that he suffers from bipolar disorder. David's manager wants to fire him because of concerns that David will become aggressive and violent when he enters a manic phase of his illness. David's manager has no grounds to fire him unless Dave actually threatens someone or engages in violent behavior.

More on workplace violence in Chapter 11.

Affirmative action

If you have a qualifying disability, your employer cannot discriminate against you. Nor can your employer fire you for complaining that you've been discriminated against because of your disability. But that does not mean your employer has to give you preferential treatment in hiring or job assignments. Nor does your employer have to show that it made an effort to recruit people with disabilities, or that a certain percentage of its workforce is disabled.

Conclusion

Don't make the classic mistake of failing to ask for an accommodation when you need one. And don't make the mistake of assuming that an accommodation is too expensive or burdensome for your employer. A better strategy is to figure out what accommodations you need to do your job and ask for them up front. Most disabilities can be accommodated if you and your employer work together in good faith. If you wait until your disability has resulted in poor job performance, you risk being fired. It will do you no good to assert that you should have received an accommodation that you never asked for.

9. INVESTIGATIONS

During the course of your employment, you might find yourself called down to the Human Resources Department because your employer seeks to interview you as part of a company investigation. Your company has initiated an investigation because it believes that an employee has violated the company's code of conduct. Examples of such violations include stealing, fighting, bullying, financial fraud, cheating on travel and expense reports, misusing proprietary information, racist comments and sexual harassment. In such an investigation, you could be the complainant, the accused or a witness.

Whatever your role, it is important to understand how these investigations work.

Why employers do investigations of employee wrongdoing

Companies do investigations of employee wrongdoing for three principal reasons: fairness, legal protection and compliance. Before a company takes disciplinary action against an employee, it wants to make sure it has the facts supporting such an action. If the company takes disciplinary action and it is challenged in court as discriminatory, the company wants to make sure it can defend its action. Certain laws require the company to conduct an investigation when there is an allegation of employee wrongdoing.

Who does the investigations

In general, investigations are carried out by a team, including human resources professionals, security personnel and lawyers. Depending on the nature of the alleged wrongdoing, auditors, accountants, risk managers, psychologists and other experts may be involved.

What sources of information spark investigations

Your company could initiate an investigation as a result of a complaint from an employee, an employee's relative or acquaintance, a vendor or a customer. For example, a vendor could claim that he was double billed by the company's account manager. Or a scorned lover could claim that an executive cheated on his travel expense accounts.

Your company might be contacted by a law enforcement agency, including the local or state police, the Federal Bureau of Investigation (FBI), the Internal Revenue Service (IRS), Immigration and Customs Enforcement (ICE) and the Drug Enforcement Administration (DEA). For example, ICE could inform the company that an employee had a forged driver's license and passport. Or the DEA could inform the company that one of its employees is a suspected drug dealer.

Your company might find out about employee misconduct through the press or social media. The local newspaper might have a piece on a bar fight involving company employees. Or an employee might boast in his social media account about his neo-Nazi tendencies.

Most companies have vehicles by which employees can voice their concerns. For example, a company may receive an anonymous tip through a hotline. Or an employee may take advantage of a company's open door policy to claim that his manager is a bully.

The investigation follows a plan

If you are called for an interview as part of an investigation, it's natural to ask, "Why me?" "Are they randomly interviewing people on a fishing expedition?" On the contrary, the investigative team focuses on a specific question and formulates a specific plan to answer that question.

The investigative team first gathers data. This includes company documents, the contents of employees' computer hard drives, websites visited, email accounts, phone and travel records, legally recorded conversations, the contents of file cabinets and desks, surveillance video footage, and drug and explosive swabs. It may also include criminal records, credit reports, gun ownership records, driving records, personnel files and information from local police. Employees give the company permission to access some of these sources of information at the time of hire. Other types of information are the company's own property and still others are publicly available. Employees who are involved in an investigation will not have a legal right to keep these sources of information private. Tax filings, bank records and medical records, on the other hand, are accessible to the company's investigators only with a court order.

Once the team has gathered the relevant data, it then interviews those individuals who have relevant information. This includes current and former employees, managers, vendors and customers, as well as people unaffiliated with company. The interviews may lead the investigative team to check out additional data.

The company's team interviewed Amy as part of an investigation of allegations that William, another company employee, was dealing drugs in the parking lot. The team interviewed Amy because she took smoking breaks with William. In her interview, Amy claimed that she never saw William dealing drugs, that she never herself used drugs and that she found drug use morally reprehensible. Doubting Amy's credibility, the team examined her emails on the company's server. They found several email messages in which she told a friend that William was dealing drugs in the parking lot. The investigative team in this case was legally entitled to access Amy's email account.

Having gathered data and interviewed individuals, the investigative team may then decide to engage in surveillance. The surveillance may involve following an employee suspected of continued wrongdoing. Or the team may use bodyguards to follow an employee who has been threatened in order to ensure that he remains unharmed.

Your rights and responsibilities as a witness

If you're called to an interview as part of an investigation, you should be told whether you are being accused of any wrongdoing or whether you're just being asked to assist the investigators as a witness. If you're called solely as a witness, then you have certain rights and responsibilities.

You have the right to be told who is interviewing you. All the investigators attending the interview should identify themselves by name and position. If they don't all identify themselves, you should ask.

You cannot refuse to be interviewed at all. If you want to leave during the course of an interview, you can do so, but you will be expected to resume within a reasonable time. Even after your initial interview is complete, you could be called back again.

Your manager or other employees cannot retaliate against you for participating as a witness in the investigation. However, if you've done something wrong and it's uncovered during the investigation, you could be disciplined for your wrongdoing even if you weren't the original target.

As an employee, you are required to cooperate with the company's investigation. That means giving complete, truthful, non-evasive answers. That means offering additional relevant information even if you're not directly asked. If you are uncooperative, you risk being terminated. You cannot be asked to take a polygraph test to assess the veracity of your answers. Even if you volunteered to undergo a polygraph test, the investigators could not use it.

The company is investigating an allegation that employees in the accounting department, having failed to receive the quarterly cost and volume data for some product lines, made up the numbers in order to complete a required quarterly profit-and-loss statement. Matt was a manager in the accounting department. He was not directly responsible for the profit-and-loss computations, but he supervised those who did. Matt was called as a witness in the company's investigation. When asked what he knew, Matt claimed to be completely shocked that such data manipulation could have occurred on his watch. However, other witnesses testified that Matt had repeatedly warned at staff meetings that heads would roll if a quarterly profit-and-loss report was not filed on time. According to other witnesses, Matt knew that some of the product lines were running into problems getting their cost and volume data in on time. Records showed that Matt was in the department several years ago when another employee was found to have fudged the profit-and-loss numbers. The investigators concluded that Matt knew or should have known about the data manipulation. Matt's failure to be forthcoming led to his being disciplined.

Whatever transpires during the interview you must keep confidential. The investigators may create a record of the interview by tape recording, transcript or notes. You will not have access to these records or to any investigative report that the team later produces. However, you might be asked to sign a statement that summarizes what you said during the interview. Before signing the statement, make absolutely sure that it accurately reflects what you said. If it doesn't, then edit it. Once you sign the statement, ask for a copy.

The investigative team can ask you about your duties and responsibilities, and what you know about the alleged wrongdoing. They may show you documents, such as emails or financial records, and ask you questions about them. They will not give you copies to keep. The interviewers might ask you to confirm or deny a particular fact without revealing their sources of information.

The team is trying to put together the pieces of a puzzle. The interviewers can ask you not only what facts you know, but also your opinions. They can even ask you to speculate about what happened or who is responsible. They will not only be listening to what you say, but they will also be observing your body language and demeanor.

Your rights and responsibilities as the complainant

If you're the complainant, all the rights and responsibilities of a witness apply just as well to you. But there is more.

Your complaint will be ineffective if it is vague and nonspecific. You can't simply allege, for example, that "there has been cheating on travel expense reports." You need to back up your allegations with specific information. Much more compelling would be an allegation that a specific employee charged the company for three nights in a hotel in Reno to see clients when the company has no clients in Nevada. The specific information will permit the investigative team to determine whether the allegation can be verified independently. It will allow the team to determine whether other witnesses need to be interviewed.

> *Hector filed a complaint against his manager Norman, alleging bullying. Hector stated that Norman regularly teased, humiliated and heckled two employees, Julie and Whitney, at Wednesday morning staff meetings. Specifically, Norman regularly admonished Julie, "Don't have any donuts, you're already too fat." He routinely called Whitney "witless." Hector was concerned that he would be Norman's next victim. Based on Hector's specific allegations, the company investigators had something to verify. They could determine if other witnesses observed Norman engaging in such conduct at staff meetings. They could inquire whether Norman taunted or gave derogatory nicknames to other employees in other situations. Had Hector alleged only that Norman was a bully, the investigation may have gone nowhere.*

If you bring a complaint, you may find the company's investigation to be a frustrating experience. If you complain about another employee's misconduct that specifically harms you, the company will inform you that the misconduct has stopped. For example, you might be told only that the wrongdoer has left the company. On the other hand, if you allege that your department was host to a money laundering operation, the company will have no obligation to share with you what it learned from the investigation. You may receive no more than a brief "Thank you for bringing this to our attention."

> Cynthia complained that her manager Bruce was sexually harassing her. Bruce was powerful and popular in the company. He was successful, competent, and brought in a lot of business. Cynthia made it clear to the investigators that she did not want Bruce to be fired. She did not want to become the pariah who was instrumental in the downfall of such a popular person. When the investigators looked into the matter, they found out Bruce had propositioned several other employees, sending them lewd emails. The other employees had not complained about him because they feared retaliation from such a powerful manager. Based on the seriousness and duration of the harassment, as well as the number of employees harassed, the company decided to fire Bruce.

Your rights and responsibilities as the accused

If you are accused of a wrongdoing that is likely to involve a criminal offense – such as rape, assault or financial fraud – you should consult an attorney before you have any interviews. Anything you say in the interview can and may be turned over to law enforcement authorities. Any admissions you make will be cast in concrete. In a subsequent criminal hearing, you can't announce, "Well, I just said that to the human resources rep, but I didn't mean it." In cases involving alleged criminal wrongdoing, your attorney may advise you to resign immediately from your job. Once you've left the company, the investigators will have no leverage to make you undergo an interview. That way, you may avoid creating a damaging record that would come out in the interview.

If you're accused of misconduct that is not a criminal offense, but is likely to get you fired, you may also want to talk to an attorney. The attorney may request that he be present in any interview. While the company has no legal obligation to grant such a request, it may allow your attorney to attend so long as he does not answer the questions for you. Even if your attorney cannot be present at your interview, he can still prepare you. He can help you strategize about the best way to present your story.

Paul was accused of violating company guidelines by spending tens of thousands of dollars on alcoholic beverages at client dinners. Paul's expense reports routinely included charges for $2,000 bottles of wine from Côte de Nuits, France. Paul's attorney advised him to put the expenses in the context of the directives from the head of the company. The attorney helped Paul go through his emails to find statements from the CEO to *"spare no expense to keep these clients in the company," and "the company will not be able to meet its quarterly profit targets without these clients." The attorney also encouraged Paul to marshal evidence that other executives entertained top clients in a similarly lavish manner.*

By the time you're interviewed, the investigative team will likely have most of the facts that it intends to rely upon. At that point, the team will be seeking a confirmation or denial on your part. You will be presented with all the facts behind the allegations, but not the sources of the information. You will be permitted to review any documents that the investigators have compiled, but you will not be entitled to copies.

During the interview, you will have the opportunity to respond to each allegation. You will be able to suggest additional witnesses, to point to additional documents or to suggest any other line of investigation that could help your case. Like any other witness, you will have the right to bring these additional lines of investigation to the team's attention after the interview.

When you're interviewed, you should be truthful. If you're not truthful, the chances are that the company has the resources to determine that you were lying. If you're caught lying during the interview, you can be fired even if you did not engage in the misconduct that was initially alleged. Refusing to answer a question may not help you, either. From an investigative point of view, it's no different than lying. In the case of a serious offense, you could be fired for refusing to implicate other employees.

After the investigation is complete, your employer will determine whether you should be disciplined or discharged. In making its determination, the company will consider several factors, including the seriousness of the offense, whether it was intentional or simply a mistake, whether it was an isolated instance or pattern of misconduct, whether you showed remorse and whether you gained a financial advantage. It will also consider how long you've been with the company, your job performance, your rank, your interactions with customers, your financial responsibilities and other aspects of your job. The company will further consider the impact of your misconduct on its client relations, its reputation, its financial position and its legal liability. Finally, if other employees have engaged in the same misconduct, the company may consider how it treated them.

Once the investigation is complete and the company has determined whether you will be disciplined or fired, it will take a series of additional steps to close the case. The investigative team's final report will be filed in the company's legal department, its human resources department or its security division. If your wrongdoing involved violations of certain regulations or criminal conduct, your employer may have to report the incident to the relevant regulatory agencies or law enforcement authorities. If conduct involved misappropriation of funds or proprietary information, the company may decide to sue you to collect damages.

If you are terminated, your departure will be announced to your colleagues and your clients. The reasons for your departure will not be shared, except with people who have a business need to know. If you have any licenses, the company may have to report your termination to the relevant licensing boards. More on terminations in Chapters 12, 13 and 14.

Conclusion

If you are a witness, your primary obligation is to cooperate during the investigation and keep the matter confidential. If you are the complainant, you need to know whether the illegal or improper conduct has stopped. The punishment of the wrongdoer is not your concern. If you are the accused and you are disciplined or terminated, it's essential that you understand what you did, how you got into trouble and how you're going to prevent it from happening again.

Whether you are a witness, the complainant or the accused, you need to understand that the investigative team represents the company and not any one individual. The team is not there to protect you.

10. SEXUAL HARASSMENT

As an employee, you need to know what types of conduct can lead to an allegation of sexual harassment. Dispel yourself of the notion that only overtly sexual behaviors constitute sexual harassment. Don't think that conduct considered inoffensive by most women cannot cross the line into sexual harassment.

Don't fall into the trap that some behaviors are not, strictly speaking, considered illegal. Companies now have policies on sexual harassment that are far stricter than the law. They want to protect themselves against damaging publicity. They want to maintain their reputation as a workplace friendly to women. They want to avoid costly and disruptive litigation not only against the company, but also against individual managers, even if they ultimately prevail.

And don't throw up your hands and say, "Everything can be sexual harassment, even excusing yourself to go to the bathroom." A reference to a scene in a movie or a compliment about a flattering tie can fit entirely within the bounds of appropriate adult conversation. Humor can be an effective management tool. The critical issue is when a particular behavior crosses the boundary of what should and should not be said or done in the workplace.

Who can be sexually harassed

The vast majority of sexual harassment cases involve a male harassing a female. However, anyone can be harassed or be the harasser, regardless of gender, sexual orientation, age, nationality or physical appearance.

If a manager favors one employee because he desires a sexual relationship with her or because she is unusually attractive, then another employee could be put at a disadvantage in pay, promotion or job assignments. When that happens, the disadvantaged employee has a legitimate complaint against the manager even though she is not being sexually harassed.

Where can someone be sexually harassed

Sexual harassment can occur anywhere in the workplace, including the lunchroom, the parking lot, the restroom or the break room. It can occur at a work-related event, including parties and award ceremonies, on or off the premises. And it can occur at a non-work related event outside the workplace if there is some connection to the workplace.

Four employees – Tom, Dick, Harry and Jane – work as a team to service the needs of an important customer. While Tom, Dick and Harry are attending a tennis match, Tom and Dick discuss in great detail Jane's unattractive physical attributes and nonexistent sex life. The following day, Harry goes into the office and repeats the entire conversation to Jane, who is devastated. Jane does not see how she can work with Tom, Dick and Harry in the future, especially in a team that requires such close cooperation. The company could side with Jane and fire Tom, Dick and Harry.

Sexual harassment that is not overtly sexual

Depending on the context, apparently sex-neutral behaviors can turn into sexual harassment. Any employee can yell at any other employee, but when a man yells at a woman, this apparently sex-neutral conduct can cross the line into sexual harassment. Any employee can intentionally exclude another employee from meetings or email chains, but when a man tunes out a woman, this apparently sex-neutral conduct can likewise cross the line into sexual harassment. If a male employee confers the nickname "Cutie" on a female employee, the conduct is overtly sexual. But if a male nicknames a female "Dumb-Dumb," this apparently sex-neutral conduct can still constitute sexual harassment.

The same applies to cruel and invasive gossip; invading another employee's personal space, hovering over her desk or going through her personal belongings; mocking, imitating or embarrassing another employee; and asking for personal favors on non-work related matters.

Overt sexual harassment

Overt sexual harassment includes unwelcome sexual advances, requests for sexual favors, or any other physical or verbal conduct of a sexual nature that adversely affects an individual's job or creates an intimidating, hostile or oppressive work environment. Unwelcome conduct is anything that the female employee did not want, appreciate or seek out. Sometimes the employee doesn't complain about unwelcome sexual harassment because she is afraid of retaliation.

39-year-old Selma had been sleeping with her 63-year-old boss Ray for the past five years. She never complained because Ray made it clear that if she did so, he would fire her. Finally, when she couldn't stand it any longer, Selma decided to bring a complaint of sexual harassment. Ray countered that it was a consensual relationship and that Selma never protested or refused his advances. The company, however, believed Selma in light of the difference in ages, the vast difference in salary and the fact that Selma was a single mother with few other job prospects. Ray was fired.

A comment about a female employee's butt is overt sexual harassment. So are comments or questions about your own sex life or anyone else's; jokes with sexual innuendo; jokes about menopause, menstruation, pregnancy, infertility or mothers-in-law; dumb blond jokes; and staring at a woman's breasts when you're talking to her.

Pornography constitutes overt sexual harassment even if you think you're keeping it out of sight on your computer. Another employee could pass by when you're viewing it, and the IT team will see it when they are performing system updates or replacing hard drives.

A male employee who engages in sexual stalking can be accused of overt sexual harassment. This includes aggressive flirting, unwelcome touching even as a sign of affection, giving intimate gifts such as perfume or underwear, and making phone calls during non-business hours for non-business reasons.

Sarah is about to make a major presentation to a group of potential high net-worth clients. Her boss introduces her this way: "And now we're going to hear from the attractive and radiant Ms. Smith." Her boss' introduction undermines Sarah's professionalism and makes it difficult for the clients to take her seriously.

Harold is head of a group that finances car dealerships. Some of the group's clients have made it clear that they appreciate attractive female company other than their wives. Harold assigns Gwen to entertain these clients not because she has done the work on the specific loans, but because she is the most attractive member of the group.

Laura's manager tells her, "I can't believe that you can be a good mother and still spend so many hours at the office." Laura's manager is undermining her. What he is really saying is that Laura cannot do both.

The two male junior attorneys in the law department were launching spitballs, one of which hit Elaine. She complained to her manager, who responded, "Get over it. Boys will be boys." Elaine's manager expects such juvenile behavior among men. The correct response would have been, "That's unacceptable. I'll make sure it never happens again."

The fragile victim

What most women might consider inoffensive could still be considered offensive by others as a result of their own life experiences.

Arthur, Zach and Ling were waiting for their manager to arrive at the staff meeting. Arthur and Zach had an extended, appropriate conversation about a date rape scene in a recently released film. Ling, who was a captive audience to the conversation, had been date raped the month before. She was highly offended and complained about being sexually harassed. It is unlikely that the company would fire Arthur or Zach, but it would counsel them to avoid content that others could be highly sensitive to.

Sexual harassment is about power and control

Sometimes a sexual harasser is a predator. He preys on vulnerable people. At other times, sexual harassment is a form of hazing. Still other people simply don't understand that what might be appropriate in a social setting is inappropriate in the workplace. Some sexual harassers actually want sex. But in the vast majority of cases, it's not about sex, but about power and control.

The sexual harasser makes his victim feel uncomfortable. His harassment robs energy that the victim could be utilizing to do her job effectively or advance in the workplace. In that way, harassment decreases competition. It makes the harasser appear powerful.

In fact, sexual harassment can be so successful in some workplaces that it becomes an accepted mode of operation. Some men learn that sexual harassment can be a very effective way to eliminate the competition.

Opportunities for advancement in the company were scarce. When a job promotion opened up, Ben and John used every aggressive, underhanded technique to try to convince the head of the department to elevate them. Maria lobbied hard for the job. She sent numerous memos to the boss outlining her accomplishments, attempting to demonstrate that she was the most competent and productive. Ben and John were furious. They started a whisper campaign in the department that Maria was embroiled in an abusive relationship, that her husband sometimes beat her and on other occasions forbade her from leaving the house. Ben was promoted.

Fatima was widely regarded as next in line to be department head. Jerome, who was relatively new in the department but viewed himself as a superstar, wanted the job. He methodically spread rumors that Fatima was a frustrated old maid and a ball-busting bitch who had nothing else in her life. Without a shred of evidence, he claimed that everyone in the department would quit if Fatima became the new boss. The division head, without performing any independent inquiry, decided it would be too risky to promote Fatima and instead tapped Jerome as the safe choice.

Dating

Sexual relations between peers can be legal and welcome. That said, dating in the workplace is generally a bad idea. At some point during the course of the dating relationship, one of the employees may want to break up, while the other wants to keep the relationship going. If the employee who doesn't want to break up keeps aggressively pursuing the other employee, it becomes sexual harassment.

Sexual relations between a manager and a subordinate are another story. The relationship is presumed to be unwelcome unless there is strong evidence to the contrary. Most companies, in fact, prohibit all managers from having sexual relations with their subordinates. Such relationships raise issues of favoritism and the inability of the manager to impartially evaluate the subordinate. The manager may breach the company's rules of confidentiality, telling his subordinate lover things she is not entitled to know.

Empty defenses to complaints of sexual harassment

The only good defense to a charge of sexual harassment is that the facts alleged didn't happen.

Employees who are charged with sexual harassment often fall into the trap of admitting the facts while offering excuses. These excuses are empty defenses.

It does no good to claim that you didn't intend to hurt anyone's feelings. Nor will it help to contend that the victim dressed in a sexually provocative way or otherwise "asked for it." Claiming ignorance of the law won't get you anywhere.

It's useless to argue that you had a constitutionally protected right of free speech to tell a raunchy joke. Asserting that you are an equal opportunity harasser – that you tell off-color jokes about Catholics and Indians, too – won't get you a pass. And don't waste your time insisting that you came from a country where touching and kissing were permitted in the workplace, or from an industry where sexism was rampant.

What to do if you're sexually harassed

If you're sexually harassed, you have no obligation to report it to the company. If you believe that the company will be instrumental in stopping the harassment, then filing a complaint makes sense. The sad fact, however, is that most people do not report sexual harassment for fear of retaliation.

Some experts will advise you not to notify the company, but to confront the harasser directly and tell him to knock it off. If you know how the harasser will react and you can make a persuasive case that it's in his interest to stop before you take the matter any further, then such a strategy might work.

How the company must handle a charge of sexual harassment

If a company receives an allegation of sexual harassment, it is obligated to do a full and fair investigation of the claim, to stop any offending conduct and to take appropriate disciplinary action. More on investigations in Chapter 9.

Avoiding sexual harassment

Ironically, many men believe that they could be the object of a false complaint at any moment. They worry that if they make even one random joke, a woman will file a sexual harassment charge. They worry that a woman could fabricate a story of sexual harassment, that it will come down to a case of he-said-she-said, and that the company will believe her. In fact, neither of these are realistic worries. Virtually every sexual harassment complaint entails repeated, prolonged, serious misconduct. A charge that sexual harassment somehow occurred in an isolation chamber with no witnesses, no documentation and no prior pattern of conduct is almost unheard of.

As a man, you're not a sitting duck. If you're self-aware, if you understand how you affect others, if you have empathy and if you think before you talk, you're not going to be accused of sexual harassment. You need to understand that just because something doesn't offend you personally, it could offend somebody else. Be aware that personal remarks should be reserved for your close friends. Beyond shaking hands, touching another employee is not standard practice in the workplace. Finally, sexual comments and sexual relations are a quick ticket to getting yourself in trouble.

Conclusion

Being the victim of sexual harassment is very disruptive and stressful. Whether you decide to tough it out or bring a complaint, you need to maintain your focus on your job and not let the harassment derail your career.

If you have engaged in sexual harassment, you can be terminated by your company. You can also be sued personally, in which case your company will probably not pay your legal fees or damages if you lose.

11. WORKPLACE VIOLENCE

As an employee, you need to understand what is considered workplace violence so that you can avoid being labeled as violent. You must be able to recognize signs of potential violence in other employees or managers. You also need to know what steps your employer can take to ensure a safe workplace.

What is workplace violence

The definition of workplace violence is much broader than the bloody carnage reported in the media. From your company's standpoint, workplace violence can encompass not only physical assault, but also a wide range of threats. That includes threatening or menacing comments such as "I like to kill animals," or "I keep a wall of hate in my apartment," or "I killed a man because he crossed me," or "I'm going to bomb this place." It includes phone hang-ups, anonymous letters and stalking, as well as abusive insults and hate speech. Rages and inability to control anger can likewise be considered as threats. So can bringing weapons to work, whether they're knives, guns, billy clubs, pepper spray or martial arts weapons, as well as an unusual obsession with such weapons.

Workplace violence goes beyond threats of physical harm to include damage to the company's property. It includes not only conventional stealing and vandalism, but also computer hacking and sabotage.

Recognizing the signs of potential violence

There is no standard psychological profile that will identify an employee who will turn violent. Nor is there any blood test, medical examination or written examination that will distinguish a potentially violent person. However, there are certain abrupt changes in behavior that could alert you to the possibility that an individual may become violent. These include changes in speech patterns, such the sudden onset of rapid or slurred speech, or the deterioration of physical appearance. They include changes in affect or demeanor, including scary or violent comments, efforts to intimidate coworkers, expressions of helplessness and despair, inappropriate staring, voicing grudges or bitterness or sudden social isolation. The use of drugs such as crystal meth or anabolic steroids can also precipitate violent behavior.

If you identify signs of potential violence in another employee, don't play psychiatrist. Don't analyze, don't predict and don't intervene. Immediately report precisely what you have seen to security, to your manager or to your human resources department.

At the start of the workday, Simon and Seymour were riding in the elevator from the lobby toward the tenth floor. As soon as the elevator doors closed, Seymour took a 10-inch hunting knife out of his briefcase and started polishing it. Rather than getting off at the second floor, Simon continued to ride with Seymour until they both exited at the tenth floor. Simon said nothing about this incident to anyone. At the end of the day, another manager observed Seymour's knife and called Security, which promptly commenced an investigation, including interviews of all of Seymour's coworkers. At that point, Simon finally told Security that he had seen the hunting knife in the elevator. Simon was chastised for failing to report his observation immediately to Security, thus allowing Seymour to remain in the workplace for an entire workday with a dangerous weapon.

What steps your employer can take

Your employer can take steps to avoid hiring potentially violent individuals. It can take additional steps to ensure a safe workplace.

To avoid hiring potentially violent individuals, your employer can perform criminal background checks and reference checks, review all traces on social media of hate speech, violent speech or other signs of a vengeful person, and conduct behavioral interviews to assess how an employee would react to stressful situations.

Stephen was being interviewed for a job as a designer for a large agency. The interviewer asked him, "How did you get along with coworkers in your previous job?" Stephen responded, "Well, there was a problem because my coworkers were clearly less talented than I was." The interviewer followed up, "That must have been quite stressful. How did you deal with the stress?" Stephen continued, "I kept those bozos under control by sabotaging their work." An individual who is willing to sabotage others' work is a security risk as well as a financial risk and will likely increase employee turnover. If sabotage doesn't get him his way, such an individual may have no qualms in resorting to physical violence. The interviewer concluded that Stephen would be a threat to the workplace and crossed him off the list.

To ensure a safe workplace, your employer can check IDs on anyone entering the workplace, make sure employees know all exits and entrances, provide adequate lighting in parking areas and locate panic buttons throughout the workplace. Your employer can post notices that the company has the right to search all bags coming into or going out of the premises. Your employer can ban weapons of any kind from the workplace and the parking area, even if the weapons are for recreational use or self-protection, and even if the employee has a permit to carry a weapon.

Computer monitoring is an effective tool for ensuring workplace safety. Employees' website searches and emails open a window into their motives and actions. If an employee has committed an act of violence or is planning on committing one, it is likely that there will be some trace on his computer. Employers can take advantage of programs that screen for key words and phrases in emails and websites, such as "bomb" and "kill."

Your employer can offer courses in conflict resolution to employees who regularly encounter high stress situations, such as bank tellers, debt collectors and meter maids. These courses teach you how to maintain your cool while defusing the anger of others. They focus on verbal hostility and not physical violence. If you or anyone else are ever threatened physically, you need to get security or call the police.

Your employer can take additional preventive measures once it decides to exclude an individual who presents a security risk. It can maintain a photo of the individual at the front desk and at guard stations. If necessary, it can obtain a restraining order so that the dangerous individual is legally prohibited from being on the premises.

Dealing with the trauma of workplace violence

An incident of workplace violence can be traumatic. Employees can find themselves unable to eat, sleep or concentrate. To mitigate these adverse reactions, an employer can retain employee assistance professionals, psychologists, trauma counselors or other healthcare providers. Participation is voluntary.

What happens if you think you're falsely accused of being violent

If you think you've been falsely accused of workplace violence, your principal defense is to show that the alleged facts are false. Admitting that you did what was alleged, but downplaying its seriousness, rarely gets you out of trouble.

Several coworkers reported that Richard had repeatedly told them that he wanted to kill his manager Shirley. When Richard was interviewed by Security, he acknowledged that he thought Shirley was an incompetent jerk, but he vehemently denied that he had any intent to harm her. Richard explained that when he said, "I want to kill her," he really meant, "I just don't like her."

Unfortunately, companies can't take any chances. They're uncomfortable trying to distinguish genuine threats from false alarms. What's more, it would be unfair to Shirley to have to continue to supervise someone who is widely on record as wanting to kill her. Richard was terminated.

Why some companies don't discipline violent employees

Sometimes employers are reluctant to investigate or discipline an employee who engages in workplace violence. A manager may believe that disciplining an unstable employee may incite him to further violence. So the manager decides not to disrupt the status quo despite the employee's threats. Sometimes the violent employee is a high performer and the company makes a benefit-cost calculation that he's nonetheless worth keeping. Holding onto a violent employee is a bad idea. Dangerous employees generally get more dangerous.

Conclusion

Monitor yourself. Be careful what you say and do in the workplace. Offhanded jokes or any other actions that can be interpreted as violent can get you fired. If you observe behavior that is problematic, don't try to judge for yourself whether the individual is dangerous. Immediately report what happened to management, security, or human resources.

12. TERMINATION FOR POOR JOB PERFORMANCE

There are three main ways that you could be fired from your job: poor performance; violation of company policy; and through a reduction in force (or RIF). This chapter focuses on unsatisfactory job performance. More on violations of a company's code of conduct in Chapter 13, and more on RIFs in Chapter 14.

Discipline in stages

If you can't do your job, then technically you could be fired on the spot. But what usually happens is that your employer will take a series of disciplinary steps, trying to get you to improve your performance and thus avoid termination. The three main stages of discipline are the oral warning, the written warning and termination.

Coaching

Even before your employer gets into the formal disciplinary process, it may coach you if you are having difficulties with job performance. For coaching to be effective, your manager must understand your job duties and your weaknesses. Both you and your manager need to value the coaching process. Unless both of you buy into it, coaching will be a waste of time. Coaching is not dictating, formal instruction or disciplinary action. A successful coach is a good listener, a guide and a teacher. He's trying to create conditions to motivate you and empower you to do well.

Coaching is a two-way street. You need to be prepared to participate, too. You need to explain what is going well in your job, what is frustrating or out of control, what additional resources or training you need and what you don't understand about your job duties.

Sometimes coaching doesn't succeed. You're too far away from your manager or pressing deadlines don't allow sufficient time for coaching. Or your job is so critical to the company that your deficiencies need to be fixed quickly or you'll have to be replaced. Sometimes your performance problems are so intertwined with your personal problems that your coach cannot untangle the two. After a predetermined time, your manager will tell you whether coaching has been successful and your performance has been turned around. If not, your manager will proceed with the disciplinary process.

Oral warning

In an oral warning, your manager will identify specific problems in your job performance and require specific solutions to remedy them. You'll be given a specific time frame to improve.

Andrea had worked as an account representative for eight years. She was the second highest paid rep in her department. So her manager decided to assign Andrea to four clients with a high volume of complicated transactions. Unfortunately, over a period of four months, Andrea fell increasingly behind in processing transactions. She began to send the wrong forms to clients – first an incorrect form to convert gold to cash, then a series of incorrect forms to buy and sell securities. The clients were complaining. Andrea's manager warned her orally that every transaction had to be processed within 8 hours. Moreover, Andrea was to make sure that the correct forms were always sent to clients. Her progress in correcting these deficiencies was to be reviewed in 30 days. If she did not adequately correct these deficiencies, Andrea was advised that she would be placed on final written warning, which was the last step before termination.

Written warning

If your oral warning has not resulted in an adequate improvement in your job performance, your manager may move onto a written warning. The most important part of a written warning is a specific description of what you're doing wrong and what would constitute an adequate remedy. The written warning should make clear the disciplinary consequences of continued subpar performance. If the written warning is a final warning, then your manager should make clear that if you don't meet the standards, you could be fired.

If your job performance problems entail teamwork, initiative or leadership, your written warning should give pointed examples of how to improve. A warning that you need to meet deadlines is fairly straightforward. But admonishing you that you are "not a team player" is certainly not self-explanatory. Your warning should require that you correct problems under your control. If a supermarket manager is supposed to ensure an adequate stock of Florida fresh squeezed orange juice, then he shouldn't be threatened with termination if there's another freeze down South. Your warning will need to explain how your deficiency adversely affects the company's finances, reputation or legal exposure. It would make no sense to warn you for hanging the photos crooked on your office wall if no client ever steps into your office.

Nicholas, a manager of a group of ten employees, has just received a written warning. "You have been a passive manager," it stated. "You don't know what's going on in the department. People don't want to work for you." The warning continued, "If you don't shape up, we will have to replace you." Nicholas had no idea which of his actions was viewed by his superiors as passive. He felt that he did know what was going on in his department. While several people had in fact left his group, Nicholas didn't think their departures had anything to do with his supervision. An adequate warning would have spelled out the concrete steps that Nicholas should have been taking to be more active, the precise information that he needed to acquire to stay current and the specific reasons that employees had left the department, if in fact they had left as a result of his management practices.

The written warning should describe your rights during the warning period, including your pay, your bonus and your ability to apply for other jobs in the company. Most important, it should specify the dates of any status updates, as well as the time limit for correcting your deficiencies.

Your employer's warning cannot find you at fault for taking a military leave, a leave to vote, a leave for jury duty or an FMLA leave. (More on FMLA leaves in Chapter 7.)

Nor can you be blamed for filing an internal complaint within your company or an external complaint with a government agency. But if your job performance is poor, don't expect that complaining about something will automatically get you off the hook. You can complain that the seats in the cafeteria have no cushions, but if your written warning faults you for never proofreading your reports, without the slightest reference to your complaint, then you'd better go ahead and install spelling and grammar checkers on your computer.

Conclusion

If you find yourself at any stage along the disciplinary timeline, it is crucial that you understand exactly what is expected of you and seek appropriate help. Don't wait until an oral warning turns into a written warning. On the other hand, if you've already received a written warning and you don't think you will be able to make the grade, then you might consider resigning. Resigning avoids a record of having been fired. In fact, if you resign after a written warning is issued, some companies will pay your salary during the period of the warning. If you really think you've been treated unfairly, you should seek legal counsel right away and not wait until you've been fired.

13. TERMINATION FOR VIOLATION OF COMPANY POLICY

The last chapter addressed terminations for poor job performance. This chapter moves on to terminations for violations of company policy. The next chapter will deal with reductions in force (RIFs).

A violation of company policy is different from poor job performance. If you violate company policy, you're breaking a rule that applies to all employees in all jobs, not just yours. If your job performance is poor, you're not adequately carrying out the duties of your specific job. If you get into a fistfight with your coworker, you're violating company policy. If you can't meet your deadlines, you've got a problem of poor job performance.

If you are an "employee at will," your employer can fire you at any time for violation of a company rule or standard of behavior. You can assume that you're an employee at will unless you're covered by a union contract or you have an employment contract for a specific, limited time period. In those cases, your contract will spell out the grounds for termination and the procedures that must be followed if you're to be fired.

If you are an employee at will, this chapter is for you.

Investigations and termination

While your company can fire you for any legal reason – in fact, for no stated reason – it will generally have specific grounds for termination that are backed up by the results of an investigation. While the investigation is in progress, you may be suspended with or without pay. The investigative team will tell you the facts that could ultimately form the basis of your termination and you will have an opportunity to respond. But you will not be told who complained about you. Don't try to find out what your coworkers are saying about you, or you could be accused of intimidation or interference with the investigation. When you're fired, your company will likely tell you the reasons for the termination, but you will not be shown the investigative file or final report. Your company is not obligated to give you a notice of termination in writing. More on investigations in Chapter 9.

What violations of company policy result in a termination

You can be fired for physical fighting with a coworker, vendor or customer, even if you didn't start the fight. You can be fired for threats of violence, even if you say you were joking. More on workplace violence in Chapter 11.

Any illegal drug use or sale, or any unauthorized alcohol use on the workplace premises can be the basis for termination. Even if you do not possess drugs or alcohol, you can be fired if you come to work intoxicated or high.

You can likewise be fired for viewing pornography at work, including images and movies stored on your own computer, even if you erased the material and even if no one complained about it. Your company's security unit may perform key word searches on employee computers that will detect the presence of pornographic material. Technicians in the IT department may come across pornography in your computer when they perform a system upgrade or replace a hard drive. More on pornography in Chapter 10.

Criminal activity on or off the premises is likewise grounds for termination if it presents a risk of legal exposure or damages the reputation of the company. This includes hiring prostitutes for yourself or your clients.

Lying, fraud and misrepresentation can be the basis for termination. That includes lying about any work-related matter to a manager or client, even if you believe that it was in the company's interest or even if your manager instructed you to do so. It also includes misrepresenting your hours worked on time sheets or falsifying your travel expenses, even if the amount of money is small.

Amber was a sales representative for a scientific instrument company. When a customer inquired about purchasing one of the company's high-end products, Amber's manager Sebastian instructed her to charge the customer 50 above the standard list price. "This guy's very successful and can afford it," Sebastian told Amber. "When he asks why the price is more than our list price, tell him that we just updated our price list, but haven't posted it yet on our website." Amber complied fully with her manager's instructions. The customer later found out he was overcharged and complained to the CEO. The company's policy provided for fair treatment of customers and transparency in pricing with the goal of building long-term relationships with customers. Overcharging the customer also exposed the company to legal action. The CEO fired both Sebastian and Amber.

Stealing company property can be grounds for termination. This includes misappropriating proprietary information, even if you did not use it to make a profit. It also includes the personal use of proprietary software during or after your employment in violation of software licensing agreements.

Misusing company property can get you fired, even if you're not stealing anything. This includes the personal use of company software, copy machines, printers, office supplies and telephone lines. You could get fired if you used the company's copy machine every week to run off copies of the basketball roster, or you used the company's phones to call your relatives in Australia on a regular basis.

Running your own business during work hours can be the basis of termination. Similarly, moonlighting in a job that conflicts with your current job can get you fired. A conflict can arise if your moonlighting job involves selling a competitive product or service. It can also arise if your moonlighting venture can bring negative publicity to your current employer.

During the regular workweek, Tom was employed as an accountant for Alpha Accounting, Inc. After hours and on weekends, Tom ran his own one-man tax return preparation business, which he called Tax Ready. When Alpha found out about Tax Ready, it fired Tom. His side business violated Alpha's moonlighting policy in three ways. First, the busy season at Alpha overlapped the busy season at Tax Ready. Second, Alpha had no way to ensure that Tom wasn't using its internal database to find clients for Tax Ready. Third, Alpha had no way to exercise quality control over the operation of Tax Ready. If Tom made a major mistake in his side business and ended up getting sued for it, Alpha's reputation could be on the rocks.

Unauthorized absences from work can get you fired, even if you had a good reason.

You can be fired for sexual harassment or bullying. You can also be fired for racial or ethnic comments or slurs. More on sexual harassment in Chapter 10.

Finally, you can be terminated if you give an unauthorized interview to the media about company business.

You may think that some of these infractions are no big deal and that your company wouldn't fire you for committing them if you're a competent employee. You could be right. But the fact is that your company can legally fire you for the above reasons, and many do. Don't take the chance.

What conduct is not grounds for termination

Your employer cannot terminate you because you filed an external complaint with a government agency or an internal complaint with the company itself. Your company cannot fire you for taking advantage of any of your legal rights. For example, you cannot be fired because you refused to perform an unsafe or illegal act.

What happens if you're terminated for violating company policy

If you're fired for violating company policy, you are still entitled to accrued wages and vacation pay up to the last day of work. It is unlikely that your employer will offer you severance pay. Still, the company may offer you some type of monetary settlement if it thinks you might file a complaint against it or if the company believes that it was partially at fault. More on severance agreements in Chapter 14.

No matter what the circumstances of your termination, you will need to return all company property and pay back any outstanding obligations, such as advances in wages or travel expenses. If you're told that you are not welcome on company property, you need to stay away or risk getting arrested. If you're told that you are ineligible for rehire at the company, do not reapply.

Whether you're eligible for unemployment will depend on the law of the state where you're employed. In general, you won't be eligible if you engaged in conduct that was against your employer's interest, such as stealing or falsification of records, and if your employer chooses to contest your application.

When you're fired for violation of company policy, you will need to understand what benefits you're entitled to. These include medical, dental and eye care plans, life insurance, disability insurance, flexible spending accounts, educational tuition reimbursement, and retirement and deferred compensation plans. More on your benefits upon termination in Chapter 14.

Finally, when you're fired, you need to make sure that the company has your current address. That way, you can receive not only income tax-related documents, but also future payments under your benefit plans.

Conclusion

If you believe that the company incorrectly blamed you for something that you did not do, then you should consult an attorney. The same advice applies if you believe that the company illegally discriminated against you, particularly if others who committed the same infraction were not penalized. By filing a legal complaint, you will be able to see the investigative report that justified your termination. Whatever the circumstances of your termination, you need to think carefully about what went wrong, including the mistakes you made, so that this unfortunate outcome never happens again.

14. REDUCTIONS IN FORCE

The last two chapters addressed terminations for poor job performance and terminations for violating company policy, respectively. This chapter takes on the third and final category of involuntary job termination: reductions in force.

Companies often decide to downsize their workforce. Generally a company will reduce the number of employees according to a specific plan that describes the reasons for downsizing and the rights of those employees who are let go. If the company terminates the employees but gives them the right to reinstatement if the business later needs additional manpower, then the downsizing is called a "layoff." On the other hand, if the company terminates the employees with no guarantee that they will be reinstated and no preference for rehire, the downsizing is called a "reduction in force" or RIF.

How companies decide who stays and who goes

A company has considerable leeway in deciding who stays and who goes in a RIF. It can base its decision on any legitimate business need that is not illegal, such as age, race, gender, or disability. A company will try to articulate the specific business need, such as the elimination of underperforming units, the discontinuation of a product, the increasing use of laborsaving technology or the loss of customers. Within this guideline, managers are instructed to retain those employees viewed as most valuable. A company can go to considerable lengths to formalize the criteria for terminating employees so as to reduce the risk of being sued for discrimination.

Home Sweet Home, a mortgage company, employed 15 people to enter the data on mortgage applications. When the number of mortgage applications dropped considerably, Home Sweet Home had only enough work for 10 data entry workers. In order to determine who stays and who goes, the company administered a standard data entry test to each of the 15 incumbents and then terminated the 5 employees with the lowest scores. Since speed and accuracy of data entry are important for customer service and cost control, the formal criteria for deciding whom to terminate were consistent with the company's business needs. Unless an aggrieved employee could show that Home Sweet Home never used speed and accuracy of data entry to evaluate employees or that there was evidence that managers were trying to take advantage of the tests to bump older workers, the reduction in force is unlikely to run into legal trouble.

RIFs that eliminate jobs

In some reductions in force, the company has decided to eliminate a particular job because it is no longer needed. Everyone who holds that job is terminated, no matter how competent or skilled he is. A company can eliminate a job if the work is to be replaced by a machine, contracted out to another company or done offshore. If a specific line of business or client is eliminated, the employees servicing that line of business or client can likewise be terminated.

All of the company's international clients spoke English with the exception of one client who spoke only Japanese. The company hired Hachiro, who was fluent in Japanese, specifically to service this client. When the client left the company, Hachiro could not be reassigned, as he did not possess sufficient English skills to service other clients. Hachiro's job was eliminated and, as a result, he was terminated.

A job can also be eliminated if its responsibilities are to be completely reassigned to other jobs.

Frank's sole job duty was to prepare slide presentations for the entire business development staff. The company decided to eliminate Frank's job and train each member of the business development staff to make his own slide presentations.

Lucille was hired to be regional manager of fifteen retail stores in a chain. The company sold off fourteen of the stores, retaining only its original flagship store. The company no longer needed a regional manager to oversee just one retail store. In fact, the salary for a lower level store manager was one-third that of a regional manager. The company decided to eliminate Lucille's job.

Alex was a teacher in a private pre-school. The school decided to integrate children with learning disabilities into their regular classes. Alex had no training or experience with learning-disabled children. The school eliminated Alex's job as regular preschool teacher and replaced it with a job that required training and experience in special education.

If your job is slated for elimination, but you believe that the purported business reason doesn't square with the underlying facts, then you will need to consult an attorney. That would be the case if Frank knew that none of the business development staff were capable of preparing slides of sufficient quality, or if Lucille knew that managing the flagship store entailed major responsibilities beyond those of a local manager, or if Alex knew that the school was holding onto other regular teachers who lacked the necessary training and experience.

RIFs that eliminate employees

In other cases of reduction in force, the company has decided not to eliminate a particular job. Instead, it has determined that there are too many employees performing the job and that some of them have to be let go. The company will determine the essential skills of the job, evaluate the skill levels of all employees who could perform the job and terminate those with the lowest skill ratings.

The company can use its discretion in defining the pool of employees who could perform the job, as long as the criteria make business sense. If the company wants to eliminate sales representatives who market a particular product out of the New England region, it doesn't have to include all sales representatives nationwide in the pool of employees who could perform the job. It could define the pool as all sales reps based in New England, so long as they were qualified to sell the product.

Evaluating each employee's skill level can be straightforward when the job entails a single skill, as in the example of Home Sweet Home above. But in most cases, a range of different skills needs to be assessed. These include objectively determined skills, such as licenses, certifications, technical capabilities, productivity and accuracy. They also include more subjectively assessed skills, such as leadership, adaptability, initiative, independence, collegiality, ethics and managerial capability, so long as the evaluator can back up the evaluation with specific examples. An important category of skills is the employee's ability to deal with clients. An employee who services more profitable or difficult clients, for example, would be viewed as more skilled in this area.

Your employer needs to be consistent in its evaluation of employee skill levels. Failing to do so exposes the company to claims of unfair treatment and discrimination.

The company decided to keep those computer programmers who had demonstrated fluency in the C++ programming language. Everyone else, including Diane, was slated for termination. Diane found out that the company had retained two other male programmers, Jake and Anatoly, who couldn't program in C++ either. The company's actions left it open to charges of sex discrimination.

What a company cannot do in a RIF

Whether a RIF involves the elimination of an entire job or the firing of specific employees in that job, an employer cannot base a termination decision on an employee's age, nearness to retirement, gender, sexual orientation, race, national origin, pregnancy or disability. These prohibitions apply even if a customer expresses a preference for, say, a young, white heterosexual male born in the U.S. These prohibitions also apply even if the company believes that an individual with a disability will require time off in the future, or that a maternity leave will be disruptive to the business. What's more, a company cannot terminate an employee in a RIF because the employee has complained to company management or to a government agency, even if the company believes that the employee is disloyal.

A company cannot use an otherwise legitimate business criterion to RIF an employee when the criterion is no more than a cover for discrimination. Thus, a company can base a RIF on an employee's availability to work full time or to travel so long as the requirement doesn't mask an underlying preference for men. A company can base a RIF on an employee's attendance record so long as the requirement isn't masking discrimination against a disabled person and isn't penalizing someone for taking a leave under the Family Medical Leave Act. (More on FMLA leave in Chapter 7.)

An employer cannot RIF higher paid employees if the practice is no more than a proxy for getting rid of older people whose salaries are higher by virtue of their seniority.

If you have been or are currently serving in the military, including the reserves, you should know that there are separate standards for when you can be terminated in a RIF.

Some employees actively seek to be included in a RIF because they can return to school, move to a different city or have a baby and, at the same time, receive severance pay. The company may be reluctant to grant the employee's request, as it is attempting to adhere to uniform evaluation criteria. The decision to terminate an employee in a RIF belongs to management and not the employee.

The separation process

Your employer can usually terminate you in a RIF without any advance notice. Even if you're entitled to a certain period of advance notice in your employment contract or under the law, the company can still fire you on the spot so long as it pays you for the duration of the notice period.

Your employer may instead inform you that you will be terminated at a specific date in the future. However, your employer is not barred from postponing your termination date if it decides that you're still needed for a while.

Tidy Tools informed Arnold that he would be terminated in a RIF. He was given six weeks notice and advised that he would receive severance pay if he stayed until the last day of work. Arnold was fortunate enough to land a job at another tool company starting in six weeks, immediately after his last scheduled day of work at Tidy Tools. Five weeks after Arnold was notified, Tidy Tools advised Arnold that it needed him for another eight weeks. His new employer would not delay his start date. As a long-term employee who would receive a significant amount of severance pay, Arnold was faced with a tough choice. He could quit Tidy Tools in one week, forego his severance and start work with the new company. Or he could stay the extra eight weeks, collect his severance and look for another job.

Severance and release of claims

If you stay until your last day, your company may provide for severance pay. If you are entitled to severance pay, you will be required to sign a written document that releases the company from all liability in connection with your termination. This document, which is called a "release of claims," will have a lot of legal terminology and many complicated provisions. The document will obligate you to do some things and it will bar you from doing others. These provisions are not trivial. The best advice is to show this document to a lawyer.

That said, there are several provisions of the release of claims agreement that you should pay special attention to. The agreement may spell out how much severance pay you will receive, what deductions will be taken out of your pay, and over what period of time the severance will be paid out. The agreement may also tell you whether you will be paid any additional compensation, such as vacation pay or bonuses. It may further delineate your rights under any benefit plans that you participated in. These include a 401(k) plan, flexible reimbursement plan, pension plan, deferred compensation plan, stock plan, tuition reimbursement plan, employee assistance plan, medical coverage, and life and disability insurance plans. The release of claims agreement may also include a provision for outplacement services, that is, career counseling to help you find your next job.

You will also need to pay attention to specific obligations in the release of claims agreement. In particular, you will be barred from keeping or using any proprietary information of the company. You will also be obligated to return any company property, including files, software, keys, computers, phones, badges, IDs and security key fobs. Don't store the phone numbers, emails and addresses of your personal contacts on your company phone. If you're terminated without notice, you may not have an opportunity to transfer them to your personal phone, and it is unlikely that the company will later give you access to the address book on your company phone.

You may further be barred from saying anything negative about the company or anyone connected to the company, including current and former employees, vendors, customers and directors. You may also be obligated to abide by non-compete agreements and non-solicitation agreements. More on these agreements in Chapter 15.

The release of claims agreement will require you to waive all rights to sue the company or anyone connected with the company in connection with your past employment and termination. This waiver still permits you to sue the company to enforce the agreement or to preserve your rights under your compensation and benefit plans. What's more, your rights to complain to government agencies about certain types of company wrongdoing cannot be taken away from you. If you're aware of improper or illegal acts of your employer and you're asked to sign a release of claims agreement, you should first consult with an attorney.

If you are terminated in a RIF and you're 40 years or older, you're entitled to receive an attachment to the severance agreement called an "age attachment." This document contains an anonymous list of all the employees in your comparison group, indicating for each employee his job title, age, and whether the employee was terminated in the RIF. If the age attachment is incomplete or inaccurate, the release of claims becomes null and void and you don't lose your right to sue your employer.

There are three provisions that are not included in the standard severance agreement, but that you might consider requesting. First, you could request a reciprocal provision that no one in the company can say anything negative about you. Second, you could request a separate reciprocal provision that the company cannot sue you for anything connected with your employment or termination. Third, you could request an indemnity provision. That is, if someone else sued you in connection with your employment in the company, then the company will pay your legal fees and damages.

You will have a specific amount of time to sign the agreement. If you miss the deadline, your company has the right to withdraw its offer of severance. If you're 40 years or older and you sign the release agreement, you will have seven days to withdraw your signature.

If you think you've been treated unfairly

If you believe that you've been treated unfairly, an attorney can help you. The attorney would file a complaint with a government agency or a court, seeking certain documents from the company that will allow him to compare your treatment to that of others. These documents include the RIF document that justified your termination as well as the documents justifying the termination or retention of others in your comparison group. They also include your performance evaluations as well as the performance evaluations of your peers.

In addition to individual data on you and your peers, your attorney would analyze documents describing how the company evaluates employee performance. Sometimes these evaluation systems have built-in biases that favor men over women or younger over older employees. And sometimes the systems are so subjective that the employer can give raises or promotions to whomever it wants, without regard to performance.

When the employer has separate evaluation systems for compensation, bonuses and promotions, the evaluation of an employee in one system often contradicts the information about that employee in another. For example, the document justifying an employee's promotion can rate him as a strong team player, while the employee's routine annual performance evaluation faults his lack of teamwork. If the company's documents show that the performance evaluation system is inconsistent or subjective, and if there has been an adverse effect on women, minorities or older people, then the company could be liable for damages not only to you, but also to other employees who are similarly harmed.

After termination

Even if you sign a release of claims, it covers only what happened up to the day you signed the agreement. If the company later defames you, invades your privacy or interferes improperly with your ability to get another job, you can still sue it.

Even if you sign an agreement that gives you severance and employer-sponsored outplacement services, you still may be eligible to collect state unemployment insurance and state-sponsored outplacement assistance.

If you hold certain certifications or registrations, your company may have to notify various governmental and non-governmental agencies of your termination. You will need to review any forms that the company submits to these agencies and correct any errors. If you served on the board of directors of any nonprofit or for-profit organization by virtue of your position with the company, you will need to submit a letter of resignation to those boards.

Conclusion

RIFs are very common, and companies get a lot of practice doing them. They learn how to make it difficult to challenge their RIF decisions. As a general rule, it's best not to get into a squabble over your termination and instead focus on finding your next job. However, if you think you've been fired for an illegal reason such as age, gender or race, there are definitely avenues that you can pursue.

15. NON-COMPETE AND NON-SOLICITATION AGREEMENTS

When you are first hired, during your employment or when you leave the company, you might be asked to sign a non-compete agreement or a non-solicitation agreement. It is important to understand exactly what you are signing so that your future employment opportunities are not severely limited.

Although you have no legal obligation to sign either agreement, your company may make your job offer dependent on your signing. If you're asked to sign these agreements while you're already employed, it may make your bonus or stock grants conditional on your signing. If you're asked to sign at termination, it may make your signing a condition of receiving severance pay.

What is a non-compete obligation

A non-compete obligation prevents you from working in any capacity for a competitor. Generally, "working in any capacity" means working as an employee, consultant, contractor or temporary employee. The meaning of a "competitor" is more complicated.

Your company can legally define who is a competitor. The company can impose restrictions on the industry you can work for, the city or region where you can work, the type of job you can have, the product you can make or any combination of these categories. However, the definition of a competitor needs to be related to a legitimate business interest of the company.

Your company must specify a time limit on any restrictions it imposes on working for a competitor. The time limit cannot be indefinite. It cannot be so long that you can't make a living at all. The time limit likewise has to be related to a legitimate business interest of the company, such as the duration of a current contract or customer relationship. State laws vary widely in what they consider a reasonable restriction.

Richard works for Miss Muffet Productions, a company that produces 3D animations. In his offer letter, he agreed not to work for any other company that produces 3D animations within the United States for a period six months after leaving Miss Muffet. Because Miss Muffet produces animations that are distributed throughout the U.S. and because it competes with other companies that likewise distribute animations throughout the country, the restriction appears reasonable. In particular, the six-month limit is reasonable because it gives Miss Muffet time to shore up its relationships with current distributors and other customers before they flee to another company.

Enforcing non-compete agreements

If you quit your job or you are terminated, your former company can still enforce your non-compete agreement.

No matter how you leave the company, you need to take your non-compete agreement seriously. If you violate the non-compete agreement and your former employer sues you, a court could award the company the "liquidated damages" specified in your agreement, even if the actual damages were much less.

If you find work that may violate your non-compete agreement, you're well advised to ask if you can be released from your obligation. Your former company may decide not to enforce the agreement because your new job turns out not to threaten its competitive position. If your former company decides to release you from your non-compete agreement, make sure that you get the release in writing and that it's signed by someone who has the authority to do so.

Your former company can enforce a non-compete agreement against you even if it did not enforce its non-compete agreement against your coworkers.

What is a non-solicitation agreement

A non-solicitation agreement prevents you from enticing the customers of your former employer to do business with your new employer. It also prevents you from soliciting your coworkers, subordinates and managers at your former employer to come to work for your new employer. Just as in the case of a non-compete agreement, the non-solicitation agreement must have a time limit. While your company can define the specific terms of the non-solicitation agreement, the restrictions must support a legitimate business interest.

Nothing prevents a customer of your former employer from deciding on its own to switch to your new company, so long as there is no record of your soliciting the customer's business. Likewise, nothing prevents your former colleagues from applying on their own to work at your new company, so long as there is no record of your trying to lure them to come aboard. Be aware that your former employer can examine the emails and phone logs of departing employees, as well as your emails and phone logs while you were at the company, to determine if there is any evidence of solicitation. It may also interview current employees and attempt to interview former employees.

Even if you don't have a non-solicitation agreement, you still have a duty of loyalty to your current employer as long as you work there. Solicitation while you still work for the company could violate its code of conduct.

Jill worked for Blue Consulting. Jill accepted an offer to work at Orange Consulting, starting in three months. During the three-month interval, Jill tried to convince clients and employees of Blue to switch over and join her at Orange. Blue found out what Jill was doing. Even though Jill didn't have a non-solicitation agreement, she violated Blue's code of conduct. Blue summarily fired Jill and stripped her of all pay, stock and bonus that she would have received.

Conclusion

When you start a new job, your new employer may ask you to sign a statement that you are not currently bound by any prior non-compete or non-solicitation agreements. This condition may be contained in the offer letter or in a separate document. If you are in fact bound by such agreements, then you have to acknowledge them and work with your new employer to get them waived. If the restrictions will expire shortly, your new employer may postpone your start date or restructure your duties so as not to violate the agreements. In any case, do not lie about your obligations under prior non-compete and non-solicitation agreements. If you sign a statement affirming that you have no such obligations when in fact you do, your new company can fire you.

CONCLUSION

Now that you have read *USE PROTECTION*, you're not quite ready to be a human resources professional. You may not want to be one, either. But you will be in a better position to protect yourself when you're confronted with personnel-related challenges. You will also know how to make better decisions so that you won't be tripped up by company rules and procedures that could derail your career.

Working in an organization is no different from playing a sport. You can have supreme athletic ability, but if you don't know the rules, the referee could call a foul on you and even expel you from the game. You can let the rules defeat you, or you can use them to your advantage.

If you find yourself in an untenable position, if you believe that your company is violating the law to your disadvantage or if you are simply unsure about the right course of action, it can never hurt to consult with a lawyer. As the lawyer's client, your communications with him will be confidential. Unless you ultimately decide to sue the company, it will never know that you consulted an attorney. And the advice you receive may be just what you need to turn around a problematic situation.

Whether or not you consult a lawyer, you yourself need to become a strategist. The more you understand about your company and its personnel policies, the more likely you will have a satisfying and successful career. That applies not just to next month's sales goals or to the next round of marketing promotions, but to the forty or more years you can expect to work. You need to act strategically to protect your career for the long term. You'll be playing this game for a while.

ACKNOWLEDGMENTS

I gratefully acknowledge the hundreds of clients who have sought my advice and considered me a trusted advisor. I also want to acknowledge by name the influence of seven attorneys: Albert H. Ross, Thomas McLean Griffin, Gary A. Spiess, Robert B. Gordon, Felix J. Springer, James E. Harvey, Jr. and David S. Rosenthal. They supported me at critical stages of my career. They generously gave of their expertise. They were role models. That said, the opinions expressed in this book are mine and mine alone. Lastly, I want to thank my husband Jeff for reasons that would take up a separate book.

Johanna Harris

ABOUT THE AUTHOR

Johanna Harris, a labor lawyer, specializes in investigating employee wrongdoing. She has been a trial attorney with the U.S. Department of Labor and in-house labor counsel for two multinational corporations. She is currently the CEO of Hire Fire and Retire LLC. Apart from her extensive experience in human resources law and employee relations, Ms. Harris has served as chairman of the board, executive committee member or chairman of the governance/personnel committee of seven nonprofit organizations in the arts, education and historic preservation. She lives with her husband, who is a physician and economist, in Providence, Rhode Island. Her two children have launched careers in the arts and sciences.

Made in the USA
Lexington, KY
01 November 2013